BIG HAT, BIG HEART

*The Story of Businessman &
Philanthropist Carl I. Wenger*

DONALD R. FITZKEE

BIG HAT,
BIG HEART

Copyright © 2012
Donald R. Fitzkee

Library of Congress Number: 2012906796
International Standard Book Number: 978-1-60126-333-9

Printed 2012 by

Masthof Press
219 Mill Road
Morgantown, PA 19543-9516

TO MERRITT
MARKS

Carl L. Wenger

5/17/17

Contents

Acknowledgments

It is difficult to say "No" to Carl Wenger. I learned to know Carl through my employment as Director of Development for COBYS Family Services. Carl and his wife, Margaret, are strong supporters, and COBYS has benefitted greatly for more than a decade from Carl's signature charity event, the Wenger Foundation Praise Dinner.

A few years ago Carl began asking me to write his biography. Initially, I brushed his requests aside. I had enough to do, and I wasn't sure how interesting it would be to write about an old man who specialized in equally old tractors and tractor parts.

After some serious health concerns in 2008, Carl grew more insistent, and I agreed, finally, to help him realize his dream of having his life story recorded for posterity. And now I can say I am glad that I did.

The writing of any book is a team effort. I had some good people on my team. Carl and Margaret's seven children and some of their grandchildren shared memories and were helpful in identifying people, places, and dates. They critiqued and in some cases corrected what I had written, improving the quality and accuracy of the work.

Daughter Rose Walmer was especially gracious and helpful in answering my questions, communicating with other family members, and helping pull together information. As is true of many of Carl's "projects," "Rosie" ended up doing much of the legwork.

Rose, Megan, and Molly Walmer, and Josh Wenger transcribed some of the hours of interviews that I conducted with Carl and others.

Dozens of Carl's friends, family members, and business associates responded to an invitation to put their thoughts down in writing. The insights and anecdotes they shared gave me a fuller understanding of Carl, by turns amusing and inspiring me. You can read these "Memory Pages" yourself in the final section of this book.

The book's title was inspired by one of these memory pages. Former Lebanon Valley Brethren Home Executive Director Paul Boll took note of Carl's big hat and equally big heart in his insightful tribute.

I benefitted greatly from the work of the late Richard Anglestein, who during the 1990s had recorded some of Carl's story in a manuscript that was never published.

COBYS Family Services Executive Director Mark Cunningham was supportive of the project. I completed much of the work in my COBYS office and benefitted from the resources of that office. I hereby promise in writing to make a generous donation to COBYS in return.

Floy Fitzkee and Kiersten Hoffman reviewed and proofread the manuscript, catching some mistakes that otherwise may have been missed and affirming that it was a story worth reading.

Masthof Press Designer Richard Kelly designed an attractive book, patiently responded to my incessant questions, and gracefully handled the curves we threw his way.

My wife, Carolyn, and children, Galen and Marianne, were patient with me as I ignored them many evenings and Saturdays so I could work on "Carl's project."

But I owe my deepest gratitude to Carl and Margaret Wenger. Carl entrusted me with perhaps his most precious possession—his personal story—and allowed me to tell that story as I saw fit.

In the process, I experienced firsthand many of the qualities in Carl that others told me they appreciate—gracious hospitality, generosity, encouragement, and trust.

In the past few years I have grown to appreciate a remarkable man who has lived a fascinating life. I hope you'll enjoy getting to know Carl Wenger through reading this book as much as I did through writing it.

Foreword

Years ago, a magazine published a monthly article called "My Most Unforgettable Character." I was fascinated by the reports of these people from all walks of life—most of them unknown to the larger public—and the dynamic impact they had on the lives of those who observed them.

As a pastor and "people observer," I have been around thousands of people, including some unforgettable characters who have touched my life, inspired me, and reminded me anew that the human gene pool does produce some great models. (Of course, I also have met my share of "forgettable characters," as most of us have. Gratefully, they are in the minority.)

Near the top of my list of "unforgettables" is Carl Wenger. When Carl and Margaret Wenger walked into my life some years ago, I had no idea what a remarkable couple I was meeting. Carl—big man, big heart, big hat, and big "W" on his belt buckle—worshipped at the church I pastored during his winter trips to Florida. Dinner and lunch invitations soon followed, and with each outing we received a more intimate look into the life of this intricate, generous, compassionate, hard-working man of integrity. Most meals concluded with a warm bear hug, a handshake, and a generous check to a ministry of the church.

Carl spoke little of his achievements, but spoke more of his family, God, antiques, cars, racing, and business—not in that order! I was unaware of many of the significant achievements of his life until I previewed this book.

I am amazed at how much Carl has crammed into his life. Here is a man who maximized his 24-hour days. In addition to "Wenger," the "W" on his belt also could stand for Worker, Winner, Wise, Winsome, Wholehearted, and Witty. He is a combination of television's "Let's Make a Deal," "Who Wants to Be a Millionaire," "Survivor," "All in the Family," and "Shark Tank." He is the epitome of a man who realized the American Dream, not by greed or a sense of entitlement, but by putting boots on faith and work and walking the talk. He climbed to the top, making his life not only a success but, more importantly, significant.

An old adage about cars, tractors, appliances, and equipment often is heard these days: "They don't make them like that anymore." They don't make many like Carl Wenger anymore either, but I wish they did.

Jim Henry, Pastor Emeritus
First Baptist Church, Orlando, Florida
Hebrews 6:10

Introduction

Carl Wenger has always stood out in a crowd. A lifelong resident of Lebanon County, Pennsylvania, where plain-dressed Mennonite farmers set the standard for distinctive dress, Carl at a young age chose a signature garb of his own. Whether at a crowded farm equipment auction, a charity fundraiser event, or an area restaurant, the large man sporting the Western hat and bolo tie was always easy to spot.

Carl first started wearing cowboy hats regularly during his teen years in the 1940s. Such hats were trendy for a time, but

Carl had an affinity for cowboy hats at an early age, as shown by this picture of a young Carl on a pony at a Sinking Spring-area riding stable, circa 1940.

as the fad passed and others shelved theirs, Carl kept his. It became a recognizable, and sometimes useful, Wenger trademark across several states.

"I liked them and just did it and it got to be part of me," says Carl. Back in the day when he traveled frequently to equipment auctions, the hat was a useful identifier. Someone seeking Carl would be instructed to look for the man in the Western hat. At auctions in the South, where the hats were more common, people searching for Carl could confirm they had the right Western hat by checking the belt buckle with the big "W" on it.

"Guys would come and would want to buy stuff off of me or had something they wanted to sell me," explains Carl. "They didn't know how to pick me out of the crowd, so the auctioneer would tell them how to do it."

Carl's wife, Margaret, recalls a local benefit auction several years ago that was held on an unusually cold day. In deference to the weather, Carl wore a knit cap, leaving the cowboy hat at home. Afterwards, several friends expressed surprise that Carl hadn't attended the event—without the hat they didn't know he had been there.

Even today, close to home, people look for the hat. Regulars at restaurants that Carl and Margaret frequent know to check the hat rack as they enter to see if Carl is on the premises.

While his collection of Western hats, some a quarter century old, make Carl easy to spot in a crowd, Carl stands out for other more important reasons:

• He excelled as a young man in Future Farmers of America and became a lifelong supporter of the organization.
• He started a used farm equipment business with a few old manure spreaders parked behind his barn that grew into a multi-million-dollar business with an international reach.
• He and Margaret raised seven children, all of whom live within a few miles of the historic farmhouse where they grew

up. All but one followed him into the family business, with the other choosing another successful career path.

• Spurred by a family tragedy, he initiated a foundation that has given more than a million dollars to a variety of Christian and community causes.

Along the way he developed a generous spirit and has made it his business to encourage others to join him in blessing people in need. Carl Wenger became more than the man with the big hat; he became the man with the big heart. This is his story.

1

Born Into Business

Carl Wenger was born into business. His parents, John Kettering Wenger and Bertha Kreider Wenger, owned and operated a general store in Rexmont, a cluster of houses hugging a Lebanon County hillside in the shadow of the Cornwall Iron Furnace. (Rexmont was one of eight villages incorporated into the Borough of Cornwall on May 5, 1926. Others included in the largest geographical borough in the United States were Burd Coleman, Cornwall Center [also known as Toytown], Anthracite [also known as Goosetown], Karinchville, Miners Village, North Cornwall, and Paradise.) They lived above the store, and that is where Carl Irvin Wenger, their only child, was born on May 20, 1932. John and Bertha had purchased the store a decade earlier, and Carl would spend his first 15 years there, learning to crawl and then walk in the aisles of the store, and later learning how to take care of customers and turn a profit.

Born the last of 10 children to Ezra and Amanda (Kettering) Wenger on January 18, 1897, Carl's father, John, was a forward-looking man with an entrepreneurial spirit. John was the valedictorian of the first graduating class at Cornwall High School, besting the other two members of the class. His valedictory address, says Carl, was titled "The High Cost of Living versus the Cost of High Living." In an era when high schools were new and many in rural Lebanon County ended their formal education after eight years in a one-room school, John continued on.

Carl's grandparents were Ezra and Amanda (Kettering) Wenger, shown above in this undated photo; and Aaron D. and Ella G. Kreider (below), pictured in 1948.

Born April 8, 1898, to Aaron D. and Ella G. Kreider, in South Lebanon Township, Carl's mother, Bertha (Kreider), went even further in school than her husband. After 11 years at Cornwall, she completed her 12th year at Lebanon High School, and then received teacher training at Millersville State Normal School (today Millersville University). After graduation in 1918, she taught eight grades in two one-room schools. She and John, who grew up together in the Midway Church of the Brethren, married on November 18, 1922, in the home of Brethren Elder Nathan Martin, who led a team of "free ministers" serving the Midway Church.

John grew up on his family's farm near Rexmont and later tried his hand working at a Cornwall Furnace plant. He found foundry work wasn't for him. Instead, he took a position at a Rexmont grocery store operated by German immigrant Henry Oltenbuerster, who had arrived on the scene in 1885. When Oltenbuerster died in 1922, John was a logical candidate to take over the store. He and his brother, Myer, formed a partnership to purchase the business. They received a good deal from the bank, and John managed wisely, recouping his investment in the store within 13 months.

After his initial investment, Myer's main role was operating an area milk delivery route, while John and Bertha minded the store. Initially, Myer delivered milk in bulk, pouring purchased amounts into people's containers. Later they transitioned to bottled milk. As John's business interests gradually expanded into cattle and farming, Bertha gave up school teaching and assumed primary responsibility for the day-to-day operation of Wenger Brothers Store.

She continued to use her teaching skills at Midway Church of the Brethren, where she taught Sunday school for more than 55 years. Later in life she also would substitute teach in area elementary schools on a regular basis.

Born May 20, 1932, Carl was the only child of John and Bertha (Kreider) Wenger. Pictured are Carl's parents later in life and Carl at age one with his father.

Carl in his first year of life, 1932 or 1933.

Good Years in Store

After nearly 10 years of marriage, John and Bertha were blessed with the birth of their son, Carl. With his mother tending store from morning till night and his father often on the road, Carl's life revolved around the store. "I was raised under my mother's feet," says Carl. "She worked in the store and I was raised under her feet."

The three-story frame building, painted yellow with brown trim, included the store on the main floor, the family's living quarters on the second floor, storage space for shoes and other inventory on the third floor, and a basement where potatoes and other items were kept. A two-car garage adjoined the building, with a gas pump next to the garage.

Mama Spanks

Wenger Brothers Store was set tight against the main street in Rexmont. A step off of the porch landed you in the street, which was cause for concern to a mother of a young child. As a toddler, Carl had the run of the store and its front porch, but he had strict orders never to stray from the porch. One day the temptation was just too strong, and little Carl stepped out into the street. His mother's response was swift and decisive. "I only ever got one licking in my life," says Carl. Store patrons who heard about the affair, for a time enjoyed prompting little Carl to tell them what happens if he gets off the porch. Carl's reply, "Mama spanks!"

The store itself included sections for groceries, dry goods, hardware, candy and tobacco, baked goods, housewares, clothing, shoes, and much more. Whatever the largely immigrant community of iron furnace workers needed, Wenger's Store tried to provide.

Carl was given age-appropriate responsibilities in the store very early. Instead of customers picking what they wanted off of the shelves, in those days shoppers would give their order, and store employees would pull the ordered items from the shelves. Since soap was kept on the bottom shelf, which Carl could reach, he got his start in soap.

"They tell me that the first job I was ever given in the store involved soap," says Carl. "They handed me a bar of soap and I promptly threw it out the window. But it wasn't long before I was stacking it on the shelf and lining it up in the proper way."

On the next shelf heavy canned goods were displayed, and then lighter canned goods, followed by boxes of gelatin and starches up higher, and then crackers and cereals on the top.

"So as I grew in age, my job progressed," Carl recalls. "I worked myself up the shelf. That's just the way it was. I mean, they always had work for me."

The line between living space and store space wasn't clearly drawn. The two intersected at the back of the store, where stairs went up to the family's living quarters. At the bottom of those stairs, the telephone hung on the wall. So when the phone rang for the Wengers during store hours, they dashed some 40 feet from the front of the store to answer. When it rang after hours, they descended the steps from their living quarters to get the phone.

Located near the front of the store was a commercial refrigerator that doubled as the family's personal fridge. "When we were done eating upstairs and had any leftovers," Carl remembers, "I had to take them down the steps and the whole length of the store to put them in the refrigerator. We had one section in the refrigerator where we put our personal things."

The living situation improved one day when Carl was with his dad at Lebanon Hardware. Seemingly on the spur of the moment, John purchased a Kelvinator refrigerator. It was delivered the same day, transforming Carl's relationship to leftovers. No longer would meals be followed by treks down to the store refrigerator.

School Days

Once Carl reached school age, he would do chores in the morning before going to Cornwall Elementary School, and then get back to work when he arrived home. He usually found work around the store to be more interesting than school. "I was never a good student," he says. "I could go out and do things, and I was street smart, but not education smart."

One of his after-school jobs was rubbing the sprouts off of potatoes. The store would keep a truckload of potatoes in the coolness of the basement and bring them up for display, as needed. Over time the potatoes would sprout in the bin. It was Carl's responsibility to keep enough potatoes "sprouted" and ready to sell.

Other tasks Carl recalls from his childhood were removing ashes from the basement coal stove, keeping the candy case stocked, the tobacco shelves in order, and the soft drink case filled and drained. In the days before refrigeration, the ice man would come periodically with a block of ice for the soft drink case. Carl would tap off the water as the ice melted and make sure plenty of sodas were ready for thirsty customers.

While customers enjoyed a cold Coke, Carl pumped their tanks full of gas at the hand-crank pump. When an electric pump replaced the hand-crank model during the early 1940s, Carl's job became easier. The introduction of refrigerated cases in the store around the same time was another major step forward.

Carl and elementary schoolmate Barbara Akers were dressed to the nines for a school event. The details are long forgotten, but they made a handsome couple.

This drawing by local historian Michael Trump depicts Wenger Brothers Store in Rexmont as it looked during Carl's childhood years. Today it is a residential building. Courtesy of Michael Trump.

As he grew, Carl watched his parents serve shoppers and learned how to run a business. Growing up in a business environment shaped Carl's values and taught him important principles that would serve him later in life. One thing his father taught him was how to turn a profit. "My Dad taught me that you never have to buy anything the cheapest and you don't have to sell it the highest," explains Carl, "but in between there is room to make some money."

Frugality was another principle that Carl learned at an early age. Growing up in the latter years of the Great Depression, Carl learned not to waste things and saw value in items that others discarded. He earned some of his first money collecting scraps. "All kinds of things were sold for salvage back then," he recalls. "I'd collect bones, rags, metal, and almost anything. Once a week a man named Hess would come around in his truck, and holler down the street."

The scrap dealer carefully would weigh the "treasures" Carl had collected in 55-gallon drums placed alongside the garage and pay him accordingly. In addition to these items, Carl collected beer and soda bottles along area roads and returned them to local stores and the hotel down the street to collect the deposits. The regular ones earned him two cents a piece, larger bottles a nickel. "You could say I was in the salvage business by the age of 10," says Carl. Little did he know that one day his ability to see value in what others discarded would translate into a multi-million-dollar business.

Learning to Turn a Profit

As he matured, Carl began to try his hand at turning a profit in other ways, often utilizing raw materials that were readily available around the store. His parents set up a wood shop in the store basement with a band saw and other power equipment, where Carl could work on projects. (He still owns some of his original tools, which he keeps in a tool box that he made himself.) When clothes pins became scarce during the early years of World War II, Carl fashioned some of his own from the ends of orange crates and sold them for a penny a piece. He also tried his hand at simple wooden toys.

Using wood from the same orange crates, some tin salvaged from pressed ham cans, and sections of broom handle, Carl designed and constructed feed scoops to sell in the store. He even salvaged and reused nails from the crates.

When, as a young teen, Carl saw a chicken pen advertised in the *Sears & Roebuck* catalog, he decided he could make one himself. Beginning with a lettuce crate, he constructed a pen with a light bulb for heat and pull-out drawers for feed, water, and droppings, and went into the chicken business.

Why Did the Chicken Cross the Road?

While he later would raise a variety of animals and become a successful farmer, Carl's first experience with animals was a pet chicken. One Easter, when he was a little boy, Carl received a baby chick. With neighborhood cats on the prowl, cars on the street, and various other hazards, the life expectancy of an Easter chick wasn't great. But Carl's chick defied the odds and grew to adulthood, which presented a dilemma for the Wenger family. People fed chickens with the understanding that one day the chicken would feed them. But Carl didn't want to eat his pet. So his parents traded Carl's chicken to Uncle Irvin and Aunt Lizzie Kreider for an anonymous bird that wouldn't leave a bad taste in their mouth.

Several weeks later Carl and his parents enjoyed a chicken dinner at his aunt and uncle's house. After the meal Aunt Lizzie confessed that they had just eaten Carl's chicken. As it turned out, the independent-minded chicken had trouble fitting in with the rest of the flock. She wandered across the road to the neighbors once too often, was struck by a car, and ended up plucked and in a pot. Such events sometimes raise profound questions. In this case, "Why did the chicken cross the road?"

"I ordered 25 chicks and John A. Miller sent along one extra," Carl recalls. "I raised all 26 chicks and was fortunate that not a single one died." He began with them in the basement and then finished them in a nearby building that had once been the store bakery.

Flush with success, he improved his operation by obtaining a brooder house and ordered 100 chicks the next time around.

Hard Work, but Not Hard to Work for

Carl learned the value of hard work from his parents early in life. "My father," says Carl, "gave me a free hand. He left me earn my way. He made me work hard, but he wasn't hard to work for." As long as Carl was doing his best, his parents weren't critical when he made mistakes, although sometimes errors brought punishment of their own.

Periodically Carl's parents would buy a truckload of cabbage, and his grandparents, Aaron and Ella Kreider, would slice it down and put it in large vinegar barrels to make sauerkraut. One of Carl's jobs was to monitor the fermenting cabbage in the basement and tap off excess liquid that could cause it to spoil. While some spoilage was common and sauerkraut in general isn't known for its pleasant aroma, one time a mistake cost Carl a barrel of kraut and hours of unpleasant drudgery.

While the kraut usually was made in vinegar barrels, this time a barrel that previously contained molasses was used. Evidently, molasses and cabbage didn't get along, and the whole batch was lost. While the mistake wasn't Carl's, the task of disposing of the bad barrel fell to him. The stench was so strong that Carl had to carry out the rotten cabbage after the store closed at 8 p.m. "I had to take it outside when the store was closed or it would have chased the customers out," he recalls. Armed with a small bucket that a boy his size could handle, he lugged load after load of stinking cabbage up the basement steps and out to the garden, where he buried it. He remembers it as one of the worst chores of his childhood.

Carl remembers a similar container mix-up that was his fault. The store sold both anti-freeze and molasses in quart jars. When a displeased customer returned a jar of molasses that smelled suspiciously of antifreeze, Carl and his dad knew exactly what had happened. The customer received an apology and a fresh jar of molasses, but Carl did not receive any scolding from his father. "'Hey,' he said, 'you were working and you just made a mistake.'"

One of Carl's more costly mistakes could have stirred his father's ire, but again he didn't receive criticism. Soon after World War II ended and cars became available again, John bought a 1947 Oldsmobile. Fifteen-year-old Carl offered to service the vehicle for his father. "I thought if I changed the oil in it I could save him a few dollars," Carl recounts, "instead of him going to the station to have it done."

So Carl faithfully drained out what he thought was the old oil and put in new. Before long the vehicle started having transmission problems. The dealer replaced one transmission on warranty. When that transmission also started going bad, the dealer looked closer. What he discovered was very low transmission fluid and an overfilled oil reservoir. As it turned out, Carl accidentally had been draining the transmission fluid from the transmission case, which looked very much like the crankcase from which the oil should have been drained.

Carl doesn't remember how his dad resolved the issue with the dealer, although he knows he offered to pay for the two transmissions that Carl ruined. But Carl does remember that his dad never scolded him for his error. "I was trying to be economical and I made a mistake."

But this time the results were nothing to crow about. As the birds neared marketable age, Carl added some clean yellow straw to their pen. Evidently alarmed by the straw, the chickens panicked, and huddled together in a corner until they smothered and died. "I had to haul them out by the wheelbarrow-load," Carl laments. "And my mother said she pitied me so bad."

Another early agricultural project for Carl was raising "broom corn" on an acre lot next to the store. The sorghum-like plant produced stiff straw that was good for broom bristles. But there also were seeds to remove before the plant went to the broom maker. The economical Carl painstakingly removed the seeds from the heads with a curry comb. "We used to get the chicken feed for the store in 100-pound bags," he recalls, "and we'd sell it out five or 10 pounds at a time to people for their chickens. So I'd take that seed and mix it back in with the chicken feed so it wouldn't go to waste." The fibers would go to the broom maker and return in the form of sturdy brooms to be sold in the store.

Caring for Customers

A general store like Wenger's carried a tremendous variety of goods and always sought to be responsive to customers' needs. "If somebody asked for something twice," says Carl, "and we didn't have it, we would get it." The store bought many items in bulk—molasses, pickles, vinegar, jelly beans, sugar, dried peaches and apricots, pretzels, rice and beans, cereals, anti-freeze, motor oil, to name a few—and parceled it into smaller amounts for sale.

Recognizing that many of their customers were of modest means, Carl's parents would go to Buffy's Auction at Royerstown, between Myerstown and Richland, on Thursday evenings to buy used dishes and other housewares, which they washed and

REXMONT STORE AND BAKERY
JOHN K. WENGER & MYER E. WENGER
DEALERS IN GENERAL MERCHANDISE
BELL PHONE 19-11   REXMONT, PA.

1924 *January* 1924

A 1924 Wenger's Store calendar. Carl remembers that his parents faced some criticism from church leaders for the risqué calendar photo.

resold at affordable prices in the store. "My parents could make $20 on a Thursday night," Carl estimates, which helped make the store more profitable.

Carl also learned to turn a profit from items he purchased at Buffy's. As word got out that he had a woodshop in the store basement, local men from the mines would stop by to chat with Carl, give him pointers on using his equipment, and talk of their own interest in woodworking. Aware of a potential market, Carl began buying electric motors and tools at Buffy's to sell to local customers. Motors he couldn't move in Rexmont he sold to a dealer in Lebanon.

Fresh meat was another item Wenger's Store provided for its customers on occasion. The Wenger partnership added a farm on Race Street in Myerstown to their business holdings in 1936, and by the 1940s began selling fresh beef in the store. They would slaughter a beef cow on the farm and butcher it in the corn shed. Half they would load in the car trunk to take to the store to sell during the next week. The other half was placed in cold storage in Myerstown to be held for the following week.

The store also provided poultry, especially around the holidays. As Thanksgiving or Christmas approached, customers could select a live chicken or duck from the crates outside the store. Or, for an additional fee, they could choose one already plucked and prepared. The Wengers, with the help of Carl's grandparents Aaron and Ella Kreider, killed and dressed the birds themselves after the store closed in the evening.

Prior to the Great Depression, the store did much of its business using the McCaskey register system. Customers would buy on credit until their next paycheck. Come payday, the Wengers would retrieve the charge slips from the fireproof register box, cash the customers' checks, and settle up. "So my parents' store was the bank for the area too," Carl explains.

When the mines closed down suddenly in the early 1930s, customers began running up debt at the store. Buying on credit was discontinued for a time, but the Wengers continued to try to assist their customers and neighbors.

"My mother was known to go get a whole bunch of bulk food, where she could get the most for the money," Carl says, "so she could take care of these people. And they continued to do this until they could get the mines open again."

When the mines did reopen, buying on credit was reinstituted, but many customers had run up significant tabs. The Wengers patiently worked with customers, allowing them to pay down their debt in small increments over time, even as they made new purchases. And most people were able to get back in the black again.

Carl remembers one woman who owed hundreds of dollars to the store. She cried the day she paid off her final debt. And his parents celebrated with her. "She said she never thought she could pay that," says Carl, "and my dad taught her how to do it. After the bill was paid, my dad told my mother to take her back in the store and let her pick out any blanket she wanted."

During the war years following the Great Depression, Carl remembers that his father tried to gauge what items might become scarce and acted accordingly. Instead of buying just the amount of groceries needed for the coming week, John would buy a few extra cases of various items and tuck them away. "Then when things started getting scarce," Carl recounts, "he would go and bring up a little bit. And people would say, 'Where did you get this?' And, 'Where did you get that?' And they would come from far around because we had something no one else had."

At one point John had squirreled away a good supply of bib overalls. He would pull on a new pair before heading out to a farm sale. When people inquired where he was able to get such nice pants, he casually mentioned that he had some available at the store. "Then they would come for overalls," says Carl, "and buy their full grocery order there too."

Anticipating a black pepper shortage, John bought a big barrel of the spice for seven cents per pound and waited for the right time to sell it. When he finally took a hatchet to the barrel to open it, pepper was selling for 40 cents per pound, resulting in a profit that was nothing to sneeze at.

Sometimes during bad times, patience eventually would bring a profit. At the back end of the store, next to the hardware department, Wenger's sold clothing, sewing items, and shoes. For a time the store was overstocked with shoes, Carl remembers, but as the economy improved shoe sales began to step up. Customers would pick out their preferred shoe style

and John or Bertha would climb the stairs to the third floor to
retrieve the correct size. On their way back down, they would
erase the old price penciled on the box long ago and write a
higher current price instead.

Store on Wheels

Not everyone who shopped at Wenger's Store actually came
to Rexmont to do it. Sometimes the Wengers took the store to
their customers on a three-quarter-ton GMC panel truck. During
Carl's younger years the traveling store delivered to rural customers
a couple times a week, but World War II helped change that. "Gas
got scarce and help got scarce," he explains, "because the young
guys went into the service." When Carl's cousin, Bobby Wenger,

*Already as a young teen, Carl was in
charge of stocking the truck for the
Wenger traveling store, which delivered
groceries to Lebanon County farms and
homes during the 1940s.*

Myer's son, left the store to enter the Navy, the delivery days
were consolidated into a single
Saturday route, and responsibility for the traveling store fell to
Carl, now a young teen.

"My parents put me in
charge of it," Carl recalls. "I had
to make sure I had that truck
loaded during the week after
school. Saturday morning we
would go out in the country."

Having stocked most of
the truck beforehand, Saturday
morning Carl would rise before
dawn to load perishable items
such as baked goods and butter.
At daybreak he and his father
headed down the road to the

Sell Her Something She Doesn't Want

One of Carl's favorite stops on the traveling grocery route was at the home of John Deere farm equipment dealer Elmer Plasterer, who lived near the church at Midway. While Carl typically dealt with Mrs. Plasterer, one day Elmer met him at the truck and issued a challenge: "Carl," he said, "sell my wife something that she doesn't want." Carl was intrigued by the notion of selling something to someone that they didn't want. He ultimately concluded that it couldn't be done. Before you can close a deal, the buyer needs to want what you are selling. Of course, Carl observes, that doesn't mean you can't lead them to want something they didn't know they wanted.

Ruhls. After some 80 stops at farms and homes near Iona, Prescott, Schaefferstown and points in between, they would end their route at the Breidenstines near Quentin, returning home around dark. "My dad would drive the truck," Carl recalls, "but he had nothing to do with the inventory on the truck. It was all my responsibility."

The truck was outfitted with baskets stocked with canned goods, sugar, and various grocery items. Inside the back door were bins filled with cereal and crackers. The bread box was located on the front right. As they sold bread and butter off the truck, they filled the space with eggs that farmers traded to sell back at the store. Outside racks fastened to the truck's running boards were filled with sodas and coal oil cans. Customers would send their empty cans back one week and receive a full one the next.

At each stop Carl would do the selling, placing the customer's selected items on the truck seat so his father could write up the sales slips. Five pounds of sugar, 35 cents. A box of cereal, 12 cents. A loaf of bread, 8 cents. A dozen eggs, 12 cents.

The space limitations imposed by the truck made having the right mix of goods a constant challenge. In the truck's cereal area, Carl would stock a variety of Wheaties, Shredded Wheat, Corn Flakes, and the like. One week he would run out of Corn Flakes, and his father would gently suggest that next week he should pack more Corn Flakes. He would, but the next week they would run out of Wheaties, and his father would question why he hadn't packed more of those.

But Carl has many memories from the traveling store. He still remembers his biggest, favorite, and friendliest customers, and life lessons learned in his travels.

With all the work to do around the store, there was little time for play. "I was allowed to go out and play after I had all my work done," says Carl, "but I had enough work from the time I got home from school until it got dark, so my playing was very limited." You couldn't play marbles in the dark, he observed.

When he did find time to play, marbles was a favorite pastime, although his parents prohibited Carl from playing "for keeps." Also *verboten* at home was card playing, which was frowned upon by the church. Cards were used for gambling, which the plain Brethren opposed, along with many other "sinful amusements" and worldly practices. Unable to play cards at home, Carl walked a few steps to the next door neighbors' house, where he played 500 Rummy, the only card game he ever learned to play. Carl found it ironic many years later to find his parents playing cards with friends, when he visited them in Florida.

Church and Community

Today rural Lebanon County is not known for its cultural diversity, but during Carl's childhood, he was exposed to a variety of people. While his family and his peers at the Midway Church were largely of Pennsylvania German stock, many Rexmont residents descended from families who had come from Eastern European countries, such as Czechoslovakia and Yugoslavia, to work for the Cornwall Furnace. Initiated by the Grubb family in the 1700s and later owned by the Coleman family, the furnace and related enterprises dominated the region during the 18th and 19th centuries. While the furnace closed in 1883, ore mining in the Furnace Hill at Cornwall persisted until 1973.

Family names such as Krall, Keller, Breidenstine, Brubaker, and Bucher occupied the fertile farmland in the Lebanon Valley and the benches at Midway Meetinghouse, but Carl's neighbors on the hillside in Rexmont had names such as Angelo, Cek, Dishong, Adams, Smith, and Perini, and were of various faiths, including Roman Catholicism. "I don't know of another Brethren in the community where I lived," Carl asserts.

Carl's early exposure to people of other cultural and faith backgrounds would serve him well in life. A staunch conservative in many ways, he would grow up to be remarkably ecumenical in his faith perspective and able to relate to people of various backgrounds.

At Midway, there were a lot of farmers and a lot of Wengers. Carl's father, John, and all nine of his siblings and their families attended the church. "I remember hearing someone say a long time ago," says Carl's wife, Margaret, "that you can't throw a stone in the Midway Church without hitting a Wenger."

And Carl recalls that during his growing up years at Midway, only three businessmen attended the church, with the rest employed in farming. Laban Wenger operated a feed mill, now known as Horst's Mill; Mark Keller had Keller Brothers Ford in Buffalo Springs; and Carl's parents ran the store in Rexmont.

The church itself was a plain white frame meetinghouse, with adjacent horse sheds and outhouses. Margaret recalls a few members still coming to church in a horse and carriage during her childhood. Once they arrived, men and women entered the meetinghouse through separate doors and sat separately from each other. (The church would be remodeled extensively in 1951, being transformed into a brick church with a stained glass window donated by John Wenger and his siblings.)

Carl grew up attending Sunday school and church at Midway. One of his Sunday school classmates was a little girl named Margaret Buffenmyer, who attended the church with her parents, Monroe and Ellen Steffy Buffenmyer, and family. Born January 31, 1933, Margaret was the fifth of 10 children. Except for a few years living on a farm near Schaefferstown, the Buffenmyers lived in Quentin during Margaret's childhood.

Carl and Margaret both made a decision to accept Christ and join the church at special revival meetings when they were about 13. Carl recalls standing in the bleacher-like "raised benches" in the meetinghouse in response to the invitation given by revivalist Ralph W. Schlosser at the conclusion of a Sunday morning revival service. Schlosser was a prominent minister and eventual

Carl's Uncle Samuel K. Wenger, who was Elder-in-Charge of the Midway Church of the Brethren, sent this 1943 photo of the Midway Meetinghouse as a Christmas greeting. Courtesy of High Library, Elizabethtown College, Elizabethtown, Pa..

president of Elizabethtown College. While Carl struggled to remember Schlosser's name, he had no trouble remembering this: Schlosser drove a 1941 black Buick Convertible. Carl can even tell you where the car was parked the day he accepted Christ!

Carl's decision was followed by lunch with the evangelist at Uncle Sam Wenger's home and a short time later outdoor baptism on his uncle's Rexmont farm. A few snowflakes floated down from the sky as Carl descended into the chilly baptismal waters.

Margaret had a similar experience, but her baptism took place on the Mark Keller farm near Buffalo Springs, another common baptismal site for the Midway Brethren. She remembers the evangelist who invited her into the kingdom was named Sollenberger, likely Clarence C. Sollenberger, who pastored the Ephrata Church of the Brethren in neighboring Lancaster County in the 1940s.

Restless in Rexmont

While Carl had little time for play, all of his hard work did bring him some privileges that few other children his age enjoyed. When Carl was about six years old, his father purchased him a Rollfast bicycle for $25. When he turned 12, the Rollfast was sold for $20 and Carl upgraded to a used All American bicycle, purchased for $37.50. Carl logged many miles on the fancy bike, riding it until his senior year in high school, when he graduated to a car. He sold the bike for $50 and still regrets getting rid of it. "I never saw one like it since," he says wistfully, "and I'm still looking."

For a time, Carl also had his own trumpet, which he remembers his parents purchasing when he was 10 for about $35. His stint as a musician didn't last long.

A more enduring childhood pastime was horseback riding. Carl's father bought him a three-quarter size strawberry pony

Six-year-old Carl, posing with his first bike, a Rollfast.
He later upgraded to a higher priced All American.

named Cappy at an auction in Norristown one Wednesday evening. His Uncle Myer boarded the pony at his home a few miles
away, near Quentin. While Carl's father bought and sold horses,
he didn't have time to ride them, so Carl would go riding with
Uncle Myer as time allowed—usually on Sundays when the
store was closed.

Some Sunday mornings Carl would ride his bike to Uncle
Myer's place at Quentin. Together they would ride back to
Rexmont, Uncle Myer on a horse and Carl on Cappy. A
friend then would ride Carl's bike back to Rexmont and then
ride Cappy back to the farm, while Carl got ready for church.

Occasionally, Carl would take afternoon or evening rides in the hills around Mt. Gretna with Uncle Myer—who began work early in the morning and usually concluded his milk route deliveries by noon.

Uncle Myer and other extended family members now and again would take Carl along on family picnics and to other outings that his parents couldn't attend because they were so tied down at the store. And every now and then his parents would close the store at 7:30 or before so they could get away for an evening.

The Midway Church's semi-annual Saturday evening love feasts were one such occasion that gave Carl and his parents respite from the daily work routine. He looked forward to love feast, although not entirely for spiritual reasons. On love feast days, the store closed early for the late afternoon and evening communion service, which also included a simple meal and feetwashing. Before he was of age to participate in the service, Carl looked forward to playing outside the meetinghouse with

Carl and his beloved pony, Cappy, in the early 1940s.

Riding a Dead Horse

Lots of people have "beaten a dead horse," as the saying goes, but Carl Wenger actually rode one.

Riding his pony was one of Carl's few leisure activities as a child. But once he was old enough to drive a car, he began to lose interest in riding Cappy.

"I got to be the age where I had a car and had less need for a pony. So my dad was selling a guy a bunch of cows back at Indiantown Gap. And he sold this pony. He thought this would be a good home for him."

When the farmer got behind on his payments for the cattle and pony, John paid him a visit. Noticing that Cappy was missing, he inquired about the horse, and was told the pony had died. John took the farmer at his word and gave him more time to catch up on his payments.

Sometime later Carl and Margaret and another couple on a double date rented some horses at Eugene Heisey's riding stable near Annville. While there, Carl spotted a pony in the barn that was a spitting image of his Cappy. Heisey also had noticed the resemblance, but neither he nor Carl believed in equestrian resurrection. How could this be?

Carl thought he could prove it really was Cappy. He had taught his pony to lie down on command. So they brought the horse out. "I picked up his hoof and he laid right down for me."

That night Carl told his father, "Dad, I did something tonight that you never did. I rode a dead horse."

Realizing that he had been cheated, John Wenger summoned the sheriff the next day, and together they went and reclaimed the cattle. "It just made my dad that mad that he lied to him. This pony was on the note that my dad had," Carl explains. "And he went and sold him and didn't pay the money and lied to him that he died. My dad didn't appreciate that. That was all she wrote. My dad wasn't going to work with him anymore."

other children from church. Once he had been baptized and could take part in the service, there still was good reason to look forward to love feast. The service typically ended around 7:30, which allowed just enough time to hasten from the church to the nearby Sears store.

"I could get to Sears & Roebuck and get back to the tools section and look at those for half an hour twice a year," Carl recalls fondly. "I didn't get to buy them. I just went to see them. That was one of the few nights we had enough of time."

While Carl learned many life lessons growing up in and around Wenger Brothers Store, by his teen years, he was restless in Rexmont and longed for more space and greater opportunity to try his hand at farming projects. His parents would oblige in 1947, when the family moved to a farm in Myerstown.

2

From Store to Farm

The Wenger transition from store to farm had begun more than a decade before the family actually moved to Myerstown. In May 1936 John and Myer Wenger had purchased a farm on Race Street to add to the Wenger holdings. By the mid-1940s, the Wenger Brothers partnership consisted of the store, the milk route, a few farms, rental properties, and John's growing cattle dealership.

John Wenger, says Carl, had experienced significant losses of investments during the Great Depression, but with the store and other assets, he was able to maintain and rebuild his wealth. While many farmers came through the Depression poor, John had means. One day at a farm auction, John started down a path that eventually would add to that wealth.

Cash Cows

As Carl remembers hearing the story, sometime in the mid-1930s Uncle Cyrus Bowman spotted a cow at that auction that he wanted, but couldn't afford. So John bought it for him. Cyrus added a good milk cow to his herd. As a return on his investment, John would receive the cow's offspring, which he sold as veal calves.

With a successful business model established, John began purchasing heifers and cows and putting them out on Lebanon

County farms. The cash-starved farmers cared for the cows and got the milk. John got the calves. Carl recalls a time in the 1940s when his father explained to him that the return he was receiving on perhaps hundreds of cash cows was equivalent to the interest he might have received on a million dollars in the bank. And the arrangement also benefitted the farmers, who otherwise may not have been able to afford the cows.

John worked out a similar cooperative arrangement with horses. At one point he had as many as 185 workhorses on area farms, where the farmers cared for them and used them to work their fields. When John had a potential buyer, he would take the buyer to the farm that had the horse John thought would meet his need and make the sale. Before long he would purchase a young horse to replace the one he had taken from a particular farmer.

John had some farmers who liked to break wild colts. At horse auctions, colts that were not ready to work in the fields sold cheap. So he would buy the colts and give them to the farmers, who worked them in with an experienced team.

"My dad would go to the auction," says Carl, "and they would come with these colts . . . on a big long rope. Everybody was afraid to get close to them. They'd be hollering for my dad. So he'd get these bought for little money and, till they were done and had them broke right, they were worth as much as a good horse. He had that appreciation, and the farmers had their horsepower for no investment. All they had was their effort and their feed in the horses. As these horses matured and got good, then my dad would get a customer and he would go out to a farmer and sell the horse away. And he'd give the farmer another colt."

As tractors began to supplant horses in the fields during the 1940s, John's horse business tailed off. "When they came with tractors, then you only had two horses on the farm anymore to do the corn planter or this or that," explains Carl. "Then he couldn't do it anymore because if you have two horses with a man and take one away, he's out of business. When he had a stable of 10 or 12 and took one away it didn't matter much."

The Family Farm

In addition to the cattle he had scattered on area farms, John also began to farm on his own. Stung by losses in the stock market after the crash in 1929, John vowed to invest in land in the future. He and Myer purchased a 221-acre farm on the edge of Myerstown for $11,000 in 1936. For the first few years, he sharecropped it, but around 1940 he hired help and purchased equipment and went into farming himself.

The fertile land included lush meadows along the banks of the historic Union Canal on the west side of Route 501, a stately lime-stone farmhouse dating back to 1799, and some farm buildings— one a barn that would burn down many years later (April 1977). This was the farm where Carl and Margaret eventually would set up housekeeping and grow a family and a business.

Having purchased the farm for about $50 per acre, less than a decade later John sold off eight acres to Berry Biscuit. The selling price by then was closer to $500 per acre. (Berry Biscuit later would sell the property to the Bayer Company, which operates there to-day.) John also sold off a portion of the farm on the east side of 501 that later became the community park in Myerstown. Several times through the years additional land was acquired and portions sold off so that Carl no longer knows the acreage.

Nickel Man

While Carl's father, John, was getting more involved in farm-ing, Carl's uncle, Samuel K. Wenger, who was Elder-in-Charge at the Midway Church, decided to give it up. He liquidated his livestock, farm implements, and more at a public auction at his Rexmont farm in February 1944. Uncle Sam's sale was a landmark event in 12-year-old Carl's life. Sometimes he cites this sale as the beginning of his business. It was the first of many auctions that Carl would profit from during his life. He got his start by being willing to take items that nobody else wanted.

As auctioneer Paul Sanger surveyed the crowd that cold winter day, he couldn't find any of his regular "penny men." The penny man played an important role at auctions, keeping things moving by taking all the items that didn't attract bids. After pleading unsuccessfully for a bid, the auctioneer would knock off the unwanted lot or item to the penny man for one cent. As the sale progressed, the penny man's pile would grow, and bidders would stop by to purchase individual items that they may have missed, or that had been included with larger lots.

Searching in vain for his regulars, the auctioneer's eyes fell on Carl. He asked Carl if he would take the job, but with a twist: With rising values of items, the auctioneer felt it was time to graduate from a penny to a nickel for unwanted items. "I looked up at my dad," Carl recalls, "and my dad said, 'Yeah, that would be alright.'" And Carl was in business. Anything that didn't receive a bid went to Carl for a nickel.

"At least two times, and maybe three times, the auctioneer had a guilty conscience because my pile was getting big," says Carl. "He reached in his pocket and gave me some change and said, 'That will hold you over a while again.'"

Late in the day, when the crowd followed the auctioneers to the field, where the 1934 Dodge pickup truck, E.C. Case Tractor, and other large items were to be sold, Carl hung back with his acquisitions.

"Guys came and started picking stuff off," Carl recalls, "and I started to sell stuff off my pile." Despite having paid in nickels rather than pennies, between the money he obtained from

PUBLIC SALE

— of Valuable —

LIVE STOCK and IMPLEMENTS!

The undersigned will sell at Public Sale on

TUESDAY, February 15, 1944

on the premises, in the Village of Rexmont (Cornwall Borough),
Lebanon County, Pa., namely:

4 — HEAD of HORSES — 4

from 4 to 8 years old, weighing from 1200 to 1500 lbs. each, all good
workers, tame and gentle; 2 are single line leaders.

24 — HEAD of CATTLE — 24

CERTIFIED, BLOOD TESTED CATTLE

some pure bred, balance grade, consisting of 20 Milk Cows, some fresh by
day of sale; some close springers and summer cows: This is a good pro-
ducing herd, all blood tested and eligible to go into any herd; 1 pure
bred Herd Sire, 2 years old, a good individual with a good pedigree;
3 young Heifers; 1 Bull, 10 mos. old.

1 SPOTTED POLAND CHINA SOW, with litter on day of sale; 20
shoats, weighing from 50 to 80 lbs., all homeraised.

1934 Dodge Pickup
E. C. Case Tractor, on rubber

This tractor is the row crop type and is in excellent working condition.
John Deere 2-14 in. bottom tractor plow, used 2 seasons; Massey Harris
tractor disc; Papec No. 13 ensilage cutter with pipe, distributing pipes
and shredder bars; 2 4-horse wagons with flats, Reber and Columbia;
2-horse Gruber wagon, with box; 2 low-down wagons; New Idea manure
spreader; Massey Harris No. 4 hay loader; side delivery rake; hay
tedder; Patent hay rake; Massey Harris 5 ft. mower; Osborne Columbia
7 ft. self binder, with tongue truck; Ontario 10-shovel grain drill;
Potato Implements; Hardie power sprayer, Hoover planter, Boggs grader
and cutter; 2 riding and 2 walking cultivators; 2 walking plows, Wiard
and Syracuse; Massey Harris 2-section spring harrow; peg tooth harrow;
roller harrow; land roller; Black Hawk No. 6 corn planter; corn sheller;
windmill; straw bench; hog feeder; hog fountain; shovels, rakes, forks;
log, cow, breast and halter chains; single, double and triple trees; 2 harpoon
hay forks, with ropes and pulleys; step ladders; 4 front and 2 hind gears;
collars, bridles, halters, lines, lead reins, straps; milk buckets and strain-
ers; egg crates; brooms; grain and feed bags and many other articles.
These implements have been well taken care of and are in good shape.

About 1000 Bushels Corn on the Ear and some Barley.

Hot and cold lunch will be served by the Young People of the Midway
Brethren Church.

Sale to commence at 12 o'clock noon. Conditions will be made known by

Samuel K. Wenger.

PAUL E. SANGER & MARK HEISEY, Auctioneers.
AMMON STAUFFER & LABAN WENGER, Clerks.

*At age 12, Carl served as "nickel man" at his uncle's farm sale, buying up items that
attracted no other bids. This is the sale bill from that February 1944 sale.*

Bid on a Wheelbarrow, Buy a Tractor!

How Paul Sanger sold the E.C. Case tractor with rubber tires at S. K. Wenger's sale is another story. Good tractors were in short supply during the war years. To prevent exorbitant prices, the government had imposed price ceilings on various makes and models of tractors. At the sale that day, several bidders would have been willing to purchase the valuable Case tractor at the artificially low ceiling price. How, then, was an auctioneer to decide who got the tractor? Well, here's what Paul Sanger did. He placed a run-of-the-mill wheelbarrow in front of the tractor and declared that whoever bought the wheelbarrow would get the tractor thrown in at its ceiling price. Bidding on the wheelbarrow was lively and a tractor was sold in a way that technically was within the law, while also being fair to all bidders.

selling items off the pile and the few cents that the auctioneer gave him, Carl came close to breaking even by the end of the day.

"Then my dad helped me take the rest of the stuff home," says Carl, "and I had a paid inventory." He sold off some of the other items at the store over time.

Move to Myerstown

While Uncle Sam was getting out of farming, Carl was feeling the pull of the land. By the mid-1940s, instead of heading home to work at the store after school, the young teen would head off to the farm. Carl would ride his bike to school in the morning. When class dismissed, he would ride the 11 miles from Cornwall to Myerstown. There he would help his father on the farm until dark, stow his bike in his dad's vehicle, and travel back home to Rexmont.

On inclement weather days, he could catch a ride with his teacher to Myerstown, but he preferred to ride bike because it was faster. By the time he waited for the teacher to wrap up her day, and then walked from Route 501, where she dropped him off, through two pastures to the farm buildings, he was further ahead to pedal. So he readily expended his energy to save time and get more work done.

When Carl entered the ninth grade in fall 1946, he moved across the street from the stately limestone high school (now Cornwall Elementary School) to a red brick vocational building, where agricultural students met for homeroom and received their instruction. (It was the same school that Carl would fight, unsuccessfully, to save decades later.) It was there that he began his lifelong involvement with Future Farmers of America (FFA).

Under the tutelage of teacher Ira Shearer, Carl quickly immersed himself in ag education and FFA. One of his earliest FFA memories was the rebuilding of an orange and green New Idea 12A manure spreader in the basement of the Cornwall

Carl began his ag education in the Cornwall redbrick schoolhouse and later would lose a fight to save the building.

School with fellow FFAers, giving him a foretaste of his future as a used equipment dealer.

By this time, two factors pushed and pulled Carl's family toward the farm. *Pulling* was a desire to be more fully engaged in farming. Carl felt restricted in Rexmont. His first-year FFA projects were limited to raising 300 broiler chickens, small scale gardening, and dairy judging in Hoard's Dairyman and the South Lebanon Community Fair. He longed for more acreage and opportunities to raise larger animals. "One of the main reasons that Wenger Brothers split was because I was agricultural oriented," states Carl.

Pushing him toward the farm was a souring relationship with a cousin at the store. Following World War II, Carl's cousin Bob Wenger returned from the Navy and resumed work at the store as Bertha's assistant. From the start Carl felt Bob wasn't pulling his weight and was taking advantage of Carl's longsuffering mother. Tensions between Carl and Bob grew, and Carl began hounding his father to dissolve the family partnership and move to Myerstown. He eventually prevailed.

Carl has fond memories of the New Idea 12A manure spreader that he and his classmates rebuilt in the basement of the Cornwall School. The spreader is pictured here on the Wenger farm in Myerstown in the mid-1940s. The hand-crank gas pump behind the spreader had been relocated from the store in Rexmont to the farm.

In 1947 older brother Reverend Samuel K. Wenger presided over the division of Wenger Brothers' assets. Myer received the store, 10 rental properties, and cash. John maintained the farms and the cattle and horse business. John and Myer parted on good terms, but Carl and Bob never were able to restore their broken relationship.

A few months after the dissolution of the partnership Carl and his parents moved to 337 West Carpenter Street in Myerstown, a short distance from the farm. (They continued to rent out the farmhouse.) It was in Myerstown that Carl would establish roots and make a life for himself and his family.

3

High School Days

His family's move to Myerstown in 1947 opened new horizons for Carl. No longer limited by the confines of the small lot in Rexmont, he now could pursue FFA projects on a larger scale as he became involved in the ag program at Myerstown High School.

John Sherman, Carl's new FFA advisor at Myerstown, wasn't as capable as Ira Shearer at Cornwall, but he recognized Carl's abilities and added his blessing to Carl's ambitious plans for projects and social activities. "He had enough sense to let me go on my own," Carl says of his advisor. "He knew what I was doing was right and he left me go."

A Growing Interest in FFA

And go Carl did. He quickly immersed himself in agricultural projects and steadily climbed the FFA ranks, receiving multiple recognitions along the way. In his sophomore year, he took over managing all of the farm records for his father's two farms, comprising 315 acres of land. He carefully chronicled purchase and sale prices of cattle; costs of inputs like seed, feed, and fertilizer; crop yields and commodity prices; and more. He embarked on farm mechanics and home improvement projects, and cared for two baby beeves, a brood sow, and 17 fattening hogs.

For growing projects he planted and tended a 3,000-square-foot garden and raised an acre of tomatoes. His 24.4-ton tomato crop in 1948 earned him a $50 savings bond in the Campbell's Soup Youth Project program, which recognized young growers for their achievements.

His yield was tops among nearly 50 youth growers from across the state. He received his award the following winter at the 1949 Pennsylvania State Farm Show in Harrisburg. It was the first of many years that Carl would grow tomatoes for Campbell's.

Carl also competed in local fairs and farm shows, winning a number of prizes. In his sophomore year he was top seed salesman in his local chapter's fundraiser. He also attended his first State FFA Convention at Penn State University.

In addition to individual projects on the farm, Carl also participated in many FFA activities and projects, such as the annual seed sale fundraiser, a farm machinery repair shop, and a spray ring. FFA members and their fathers gave their time to fix and build farm machinery and implements at a small shop.

Using a ten wheeler GMC former army truck with a 400-gallon tank and high pressure hoses, Myerstown FFAers sprayed fruit trees throughout the local area each year for a modest fee. Students volunteered their time for the project. In a May 1948 report in *The Keystone Farmer*,

Carl proudly displays his FFA jacket, and an impressive pompadour, during his high school years.

FFA Instructor John R. Sherman reported that during the previous season they had applied 22,300 gallons of spray on 1,625 trees for 156 customers. In addition, they used their rig to spray acres of tomatoes and to pressure wash the interiors of broiler chicken houses.

It didn't take long for the Myerstown Chapter to recognize Carl's abilities and leadership qualities. Having earned his Greenhand Degree while still at Cornwall, he added his Chapter Degree his first year in Myerstown (October 1947), and was elected Chapter Secretary and Chairman of the Initiation and Program Committee. The following year he would be named Treasurer.

Carl carefully documented all of his achievements in an article that appeared in the April 1949 issue of the national magazine *The American Farm Youth*. The article chronicled his FFA activities into his junior year, earning him national recognition and a $10 first prize in the magazine's monthly writing contest for FFA members. His meticulous farm records earned Carl another $10 first prize in 1949 in the Production Credit Record Keeping Contest sponsored by the Lancaster Production Credit Association.

During his junior year Carl served as Vice-President of the Lebanon County FFA. Victor Ziegler, a Brethren youth from a neighboring chapter was President. Carl's and Victor's paths would cross frequently. In January 1950, both Carl and Victor received statewide recognition by earning their Keystone Degree, and three years later both would receive the national American Farmer Degree.

Benefits of a '49 Oldsmobile

While Carl worked hard and took FFA very seriously, it wasn't all work and no play. Much of his social life also revolved around FFA. FFA, sometimes in conjunction with its female partner organization Future Homemakers of America (FHA), sponsored activities such as a basketball tournament, a Father & Son Banquet, a roller skating party, and even a dance. Carl would read the national FFA magazine to see what other local chapters were doing and ask, "Why not us?" Carl was instrumental in having his chapter's first sweetheart dance, first Halloween parade float, the first chapter banquet, and more.

A local newspaper described festivities of an FFA/FHA dance, held at Myerstown High School in January 1950: The evening culminated with the "impressive coronation of the F.F.A. Chapter Sweetheart." The honor went to Bonnie A. Wise, described as "a pretty senior and F.H.A. member" in a "light green dress." She received a nosegay, a bouquet of roses, and the opportunity to dance with FFA President Clark Levengood to strains of "Let Me Call You Sweetheart."

Carl didn't get the girl that night. In fact, Carl lacked many of the traits that typically make teens popular. He wasn't particularly tall or handsome or athletic. He wore glasses and carried a few extra pounds even as a youth. But he had one thing

Peering through the windshield of his '49 Oldsmobile, life looked good to Carl.

that most of his potential rivals did not. On Wednesday, January 13, 1949, when Carl was just 16, his father entrusted him with a brand new 1949 six-cylinder Oldsmobile. The sleek, black sedan was the first in Lebanon County to feature an eye-catching new Olds body style. Carl's social life took a sharp turn for the better the minute he climbed behind the wheel.

"My dad never paid me much money," Carl explains, "but when I was 16 years old he went and bought me my first car. He just stepped right up to the plate and bought it for me." Though his father paid him a modest $10 weekly salary (increased to 15 when he married), Carl had something nobody else had—a brand new car. His dad provided some gas money and Carl put much of the rest of his pay toward gas, reveling in the freedom to go where he pleased, with whomever he pleased. One spring night in 1950, it would please him to give Margaret Buffenmyer a ride in the Olds.

Dating Days

Carl and Margaret had grown up together in the Midway Church of the Brethren, but didn't take special interest in each other during their early years. Margaret recalls one church youth activity that involved travel on a bus. Guys and girls were pairing up for the ride, and some of Margaret's friends were encouraging her to sit with Carl. Direct and to the point, Margaret rejected the idea out of hand, declaring, "He's too fat!"

But by their senior year in high school, Margaret was ready to reconsider. When Carl offered her a ride home from Midway love feast in his shiny black Olds on Saturday night, May 13, 1950, she accepted. They took the long way, stopping to play a round of miniature golf at Nancy Lou's Barbecue, on the south side of Route 422 between Palmyra and Lebanon. Margaret recalls that after that first ride home, she didn't know if Carl would come back for a second date. But the following Saturday was Carl's 18th birthday, and he came to celebrate it with Margaret. They were officially a couple.

A few weeks later, on May 23, 1950, Carl graduated from Myerstown High School and turned his full attention to farming in partnership with his parents. In addition to working on the farm, Carl partnered with his father in other agricultural pursuits. Already at age 15, a year before he had his driver's license, Carl frequently hauled cattle for his father in the family cattle truck. While still a teen, Carl also got into doing custom farm work for others.

"As a teenager, I convinced my father it was time to modernize some of our equipment," Carl recalls. They added a new 1948 Farmall M tractor to the Farmall Straight A they already had, and added a plow for the A. Soon Carl was plowing lots around town with the A, with Carl receiving half of the income and his father receiving the other half for his investment.

John also bought a New Holland 76 baler and a John Deere 12A combine, the first combine in the area with a grain tank, and Carl baled and combined on farms from Myerstown all the way down to the Lancaster-Lebanon County line, near Brickerville.

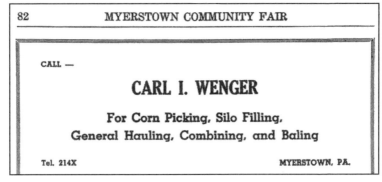

An ad in the 1950 Myerstown Community Fair booklet touted Carl's custom farm services.

One of the places Carl baled hay was on his own 60-acre farm near Fort Indiantown Gap, north of Annville. He purchased the land and barn from Web Kreiser for $6,000 while he still was in high school. He put nearly all of it in grass and used it to pasture dry cows and make hay. He sold that farm a few years later. "I had some income for quite a while from the sale," he recalls.

Carl and Margaret dated throughout the summer of 1950, enjoying rides together in the car, attending revival meetings and other special services at local Church of the Brethren congregations, playing miniature golf, or frequenting the Dixie Drive-In in Lebanon, where servers would hang a tray of burgers, fries, and shakes on the side of the Olds for Carl and Margaret to enjoy.

"Hired Man" or Helpmate?

Of course, dating often took a backseat to farm work. Carl remembers one July Saturday night when he had to finish harvesting some grain. Their date didn't begin until he arrived after 10 p.m. "I had to finish my combining," Carl explains. "I couldn't just quit and go."

"Sunday evenings I would go along down on the farm," Margaret recalls. "Before we were married Carl was farming and he had calves to take care of and farming to do, so I would go along just to take care of the calves and whatever work he had to do there." She understood that the faster they got the work done, the sooner they could do other things. And she understood, to some extent, the kind of life she would share with Carl in the future.

Even when they took Sunday afternoon walks together, it wasn't entirely for pleasure. An electric fence surrounded a pasture where Carl's dad grazed heifers. "Every Sunday afternoon

Carl poses with his parents (above) and alone (opposite page) on his wedding day. The wedding portrait of Carl and Margaret was taken in a studio prior to their wedding. They never received the professional photos from their wedding day, due to the premature death of the photographer.

I had to go and walk that fence and make sure there were no shorts on the electric fence," Carl recalls.

By September, Carl was convinced he had found the love of his life. One September day he picked Margaret up from her job at Noggle's Lingerie Factory in Rexmont, where she had begun work after completing 10 years of school at Cornwall. As they drove east out of Rexmont, Carl eased off the road into a little pull-off in a wooded area in South Lebanon Township, where they sat in the car, enjoying lunch together. Carl proposed, and Margaret said yes.

With that settled, they wasted no time in scheduling a wedding for December 23, 1950, some seven months after their first date. Explaining the whirlwind courtship and short engagement, Margaret deadpans, "He needed a hired man." Carl doesn't deny Margaret's assessment, although he might have used the word "helpmate." Of course, Margaret also had ulterior motives. She despised her job in the garment factory and was ready to try her hand at farming.

Because major renovations rendered the Midway Church unavailable until the following spring, Carl and Margaret were married in the Lebanon Church of the Brethren, with Pastor Carl W. Zeigler and Uncle Samuel Wenger officiating at the early afternoon service. Jay Brown served as best man, while Margaret's sister, Alma Buffenmyer, was Maid of Honor. Carl was 18 years old, Margaret 17.

One advantage of marrying in the more liberal city church was that Reverend Zeigler allowed a ring ceremony as part of the service, a "worldy" practice that Uncle Sam would not have permitted, had he officiated at the plainer Midway Church. A reception for 150 or more guests followed in the Lebanon church basement.

Sadly, their wedding photographer died unexpectedly before processing the dozens of photos that he had captured at the wedding and reception. As a result, Carl and Margaret never received their wedding photos. They have only a few posed studio shots, taken prior to their wedding day, to document the event.

4

Setting Up Housekeeping

Thinking back to the months prior to her wedding, Margaret remembers her mother gently cautioning, "You know, if you marry a farmer, that's a lot of hard work." While she had ample evidence during her dating days to confirm the truth of what her mother told her, she says she didn't fully realize what she was getting into. "You know, I was 17 years old and I was in love, so it went in one ear and out the other. But," she adds, "I soon found out."

Short Honeymoon

Mr. and Mrs. Wenger returned home on their wedding night around 8:00 p.m. The honeymoon was short. They arose before 6:00 the next morning and trudged to the barn, where 32 cows were waiting to be fed and milked. Margaret received her first milking lesson on that Christmas Eve morning. Before long, she would be doing the majority of the milking, while also caring for a growing family.

During the winter months, Carl and Margaret worked on renovating the large limestone farmhouse at 410 S. Race Street, where they would set up housekeeping, raise their family, and live for 60 years. Initially, they occupied half of the house and rented the other half to tenants.

Dating back to 1799, the stately house and adjacent spring house once belonged to the Bassler family, prominent early Swiss immigrants in the Lebanon Valley. In hindsight, Carl admits that they made some mistakes in failing to preserve some of the historic features of the landmark building. "We tore a few things out that you wouldn't do today," he says. But their goal at the time was to get it ready to move in, not historic preservation.

As the renovations were completed, Carl and Margaret planned to buy some used furnishings, but Carl's parents objected. "My parents said, 'Whoa,'" Carl recalls. "'You got yourself a nice girl and we think we want to buy you some new furniture and appliances.'" So they went to an appliance store in Lebanon, John did some dickering, and they came home with new appliances. He did the same for furniture.

"Dad bought all of the appliances," says Carl, "and we came home and Dad said, 'Come on, let's get back to work.' We went home and got several hours' worth of work in. That's just the way he was. No sense you spent extra time getting something done; you get back to work and earn some money to pay for it."

Carl and Margaret set up housekeeping in a historic 18th-century farmhouse.

Hurry Up!

Carl grew up accustomed to hearing the words, "Hurry up!" from his father. "Everything he said included 'hurry up,'" Carl recalls. "'Go get a hammer and nail and hurry up.' It got so that everything I did was in half a run. As a young guy I would go across town to the hardware store and I would run in and get what I needed and run back out. People would see me and say, 'You aren't going to do that all your life.' Other people would say that they couldn't believe that a guy was trying to make up that much time. But my dad just believed you ought to get a whole lot done in a short period of time. And he did. And we did."

As a result of John and Bertha's generosity, Carl and Margaret started housekeeping with nicer things than many of their peers. "That's how good my parents were (to us)," says Carl with appreciation.

Successful Farmers

On April 1, 1951, John and Bertha turned the operation of the farm over to Carl and Margaret. "He had faith we could handle the farm," says Carl. Carl's parents retained ownership of the farm and cows, while Carl purchased the equipment from his dad at fair market value, with financing provided by John. Carl and Margaret did most of the farm work, and they split the milk check with John and Bertha. Pleased with how his son was running the farm, John eventually cancelled Carl's debt on the equipment.

In addition to milking the 32 cows, which soon became 42, Carl and Margaret also had 500 or more laying hens in the early years. In the fields they put out 10 acres of tomatoes for

Scenes from tomato picking during the 1950s. In the center photo, Carl is standing on the 1946 Chevrolet truck and his father is at the front of the vehicle. The workers in the bottom photo are standing on the exact plot of ground where Carl and Margaret would build their retirement home more than 50 years later.

Campbell's and seven acres of tobacco—both labor-intensive endeavors. Carl and Margaret were among the first farmers in the area to employ migrant workers to help harvest their tomatoes.

While they had high quality DeLaval milking equipment, dairy farming was still back-breaking work. There was constant stooping to wash teats and attach milkers, all the while dodging tails that had lain in the stable muck. Milk had to be lugged in buckets and poured into milk cans in the milk house—this was before refrigerated bulk tanks.

Margaret not only helped milk; it was her job to keep the milk house clean. "The milk inspectors were always on her," Carl recalls.

In addition, hundreds of eggs from the laying hens had to be gathered daily by hand and graded one by one. The eggs were sold as hatching eggs to Mark Hershey Farms, along Route 322, near Quentin. "We would get a premium," says Carl, "because we had crossers—gold roosters and red chickens." These crossbred chicks grew up to be premium broilers.

Dropping eggs off at Mark Hershey's was a Sunday evening ritual. "We would load the eggs and go up to Mark Hershey's place. He had his office door open, and we would go in, unload the eggs, and get a couple empty cases." They would then retrieve the check for the previous week's eggs from a desk drawer, and then visit Margaret's parents on the way home.

Before long Carl and Margaret had not only cows and chickens to care for, but children. They were blessed with the birth of their first child less than a year after they married. Lloyd was born on November 7, 1951. Larry, Nancy, and Carol followed in close succession, for a total of four children in four years. Davey, Glenn, and Rosie would come later.

Children's Birthdates

Carl and Margaret were blessed with seven children:

Lloyd John	November 7, 1951
Larry Carl	December 19, 1952
Nancy Jean	October 7, 1954
Carol Joan	October 4, 1955
David Monroe	June 20, 1960
Glenn Todd	August 11, 1962
Rose Ellen	August 31, 1963

National Recognition

As their family grew, Carl and Margaret worked hard at being successful farmers. They were good at what they did and continued to receive recognition for their agricultural achievements. Though he had graduated from high school in 1950, Carl remained active in FFA as a young married man. He had received his state Keystone Farmer Degree in January 1950, and was elected to the state office of Reporter for the 1951-52 year, which brought with it a flurry of activities. In his final report in *The Keystone Farmer*, Carl reported that he had attended 12 meetings and six fairs, delivered four speeches and two radio broadcasts, sent 20 letters, and traveled more than a thousand miles to carry out his responsibilities.

With his state office term completed, Carl set his sights on the national stage, where he satisfied the rigorous application requirements for the prestigious American Farmer Degree. He was elated to receive a letter from State Chief of Agricultural Education H. C. Fetterolf, dated August 26, 1953, informing him that he was one of 11 Pennsylvania farmers (out of more than 11,000 FFA members in the state) to be chosen for this high honor. Fetterolf wrote, in

Some of Carl's agricultural achievements were highlighted in the Camden edition of the January 1954 Campbell People *magazine. Pictured in the bottom photo (from left) are Supervisor of Campbell's Youth Program Jim Woodford, County Advisor of Agricultural Education Lloyd Lebo, Carl, Carl's father John Wenger (partially obscured), and Myerstown High School Agriculture Teacher John Sherman. (Above) Carl and Margaret, holding sons Lloyd and Larry on the front porch of their home.*

part, "This is an accomplishment and an honor which has come to you because of your outstanding farming record, your fine scholarship, and your splendid leadership."

Carl and Margaret traveled to the October 12-15 National FFA Convention in Kansas City, Missouri, to receive his award. It was the closest they ever came to a honeymoon trip. As he sat among the thousands attending that convention, he aspired to still greater recognition. Each year FFA named four Regional Star Farmers and a single National Star Farmer.

"I sat out in Kansas City and saw the Stars over America program and I saw the Star Farmer and I wanted to be him," Carl recalls. But when Carl was beaten out by a young farmer in Massachusetts for Eastern Region Star Farmer, he lost his opportunity to compete for the Star Farmer award.

"I didn't get that and I cried," Carl recalls. "But I made up my mind that I was going to get up there sometime." His dream would be partially realized 20 years later, when his oldest son, Lloyd, earned the Regional Star Agri-Businessman degree. Sons David and Glenn would follow as Regional Stars, but all three fell short of the top national prize.

Closer to home, Carl remained heavily involved in FFA and was branching out into other community endeavors. In 1952 he joined the Myerstown Lions Club, beginning an association that would span six decades. While he missed being a charter member by one year, he was the youngest member ever inducted and at this writing is the active member with longest tenure.

Two years after becoming a Lion, Carl was chosen to chair the Agriculture Committee of the Lebanon County Chamber of Commerce. A folksy July 10, 1954, *Lebanon Daily News* article announcing the appointment reviewed Carl's family history, farming operation, FFA achievements, and even his "jolly" appearance, "built-in grin," and "prodigious appetite." In passing, the article mentioned a little hobby Carl enjoyed on the side— buying and selling farm implements.

5

Beginnings of a Business

Carl Wenger never set out to be a farm equipment dealer. He was a nationally-recognized farmer who had no intentions of being anything but a successful farmer. But life happens and, before long, corn pickers and choppers would supplant cows and chickens, fields and meadows would become a sales lot, and used farm equipment would become Carl's cash crop. It began innocently enough when Carl thought he needed a second manure spreader.

"We had a New Idea 12A manure spreader," Carl explains, "and when we went to haul manure off the pile . . . it would have been so much easier if we had two. So I went out and bought the second one, a good one."

Before long his good spreader caught the eye of another farmer, who offered to buy it. Carl agreed to sell it for about what he had paid for it, and got the buyer to throw in his old spreader. "So I got this old junker and parked it behind the barn."

Carl thought he was on to something so he repeated the process several times, buying good spreaders, reselling them, and getting an old spreader as part of the deal. Before long a half dozen worn manure spreaders were stationed behind the barn. "I had junk spreaders," says Carl, "but I had my money back and I had a [usable] spreader all the time." Carl was in the equipment business.

Carl began his equipment business with a few New Idea manure spreaders parked behind the barn. The barn pictured here later would be lost to fire.

Multiplying Manure Spreaders and Trading Tractors

With manure spreaders multiplying, Carl ran into an acquaintance, Caleb Stauffer, at a farm sale. Caleb wondered if Carl would have any work for him to do. Carl ruminated on Caleb's request as the sale progressed. The following week he had a proposal for Caleb: "I said, 'How about you go out there and pick out the best manure spreader and bring it in here. And then you see what you need and you go take it off of the worst one. See how many spreaders you can make for me out of that row.'"

Caleb mixed and matched to make a few salable spreaders out of the lot, and piled the leftover pieces under a shade tree. Before long word spread and farmers would stop by to pick parts off of the pile. Carl was in the parts business.

Not long after that Carl spotted an Oliver 80 tractor with a blown engine at a farm sale. While most people saw a piece of junk, Carl noticed that the tractor had new tires. "I thought, 'Hey, I can get more for that rubber than the tractor cost,'" says

Carl. He bought his first salvage tractor, parked it out back, and sold off the tires. Now he was in the salvage tractor business.

A short time later, Carl decided he could use another tractor on his farm. He had purchased a John Deere B, and the two Farmalls from his father, but he needed a fourth. A used Oliver 70 caught his eye at Keller Brothers in Buffalo Springs, and though he had to take a note out on it until the next milk check came, he bought it.

The Oliver came with a corn planter and cultivator, neither of which Carl needed, so he paid a visit to Oliver dealer Jake Fahnestock in Stouchburg and let him know that he had pieces for sale. A few weeks later a pair of cultivator customers came calling. They were looking at a tractor at Fahnestock's, but needed Carl's attachments. But when they saw Carl using his Oliver tractor to run a hammer mill to grind some feed, they inquired whether it was for sale, too.

Carl said, "Not really," but they persisted and asked what he would take for it. "So I priced it like I wanted to keep it," said Carl. A short time later the buyers returned. When Carl said he could deliver the tractor to their location near Reading, the deal was closed. "I delivered it and they paid for it," says Carl. It was the first of many pieces Carl would deliver with the cattle truck.

With one deal closed and money burning a hole in his pocket, Carl quickly moved on to the next. He was aware of a large Farmall F30 with loader that farmer Paul Groff wanted to sell. Carl bought it and took it directly to auctioneer Paul Sanger's sale along Route 422, west of Myerstown. Paul wasn't able to get a bid high enough for Carl to get his money back. As they stood talking after the sale was done, a vehicle pulled over along 422, and a man vaulted the guardrail and breathlessly asked whether the Farmall had been sold. After some dickering and agreeing to deliver the tractor to Gouglersville (between Adamstown and Reading), Carl made the sale. Now Carl was in the tractor business, having sold two in one week.

Once he caught his breath after his initial tractor sales, Carl went back to Jake Fahnestock and offered an apology and a commission on the sale of the Oliver. Carl felt bad that Jake had sent implement customers and Carl sold them a tractor, which may have cost Jake a sale of his own Oliver tractor. But Jake had found another buyer for his, and encouraged Carl just to send him a customer in return sometime.

While Jake and eventually many other tractor and implement dealers were potential competitors to Carl, Carl tried to see things differently: "I was taught that we should never have competitors," he says. "You should buy something from them and call them a vendor or sell something to them and call them a customer."

Carl would have many vendors and customers. His third tractor sale was an 8N Ford that he bought at the sale of his cousin, Herman Smith, near Fontana. "I kept selling my own tractors and leaving myself short by one," Carl explains. But before long he was buying two tractors, instead of one, at a sale, and then three, instead of two, and eventually he would buy 50 instead of 25. "We just kept on going," says Carl.

Expanding Circles

As his business grew, Carl would farm during the day, haul cattle for his dad in the evening, and then wheel and deal for farm equipment late into the night. The three pursuits complemented each other nicely. As already mentioned, Carl often sold off pieces of his own equipment if the price was right. And as he hauled cattle from farm to farm, he would learn what equipment and tractors farmers had for sale or were looking to buy. Armed with this information, he would seek out the pieces for waiting farmers.

Lancaster County equipment dealer Clyde Keener often had what he needed. Clyde started his equipment business in the village of Sporting Hill, before relocating along busy Route 72, closer to the city of Lancaster. "He had a field of farm equipment with pretty good inventory," Carl explains. "I would go buy it from Clyde and take it and sell it to the farmers."

Carl also began to frequent local farm sales to snatch up tractors and implements for resale. "He went to all the local sales," Margaret recalls. "If there was a public sale and they had equipment, Carl was there."

But as Carl began attending more sales, he and Clyde started to run into each other. "After a while Clyde and I were bidding against each other," Carl explains. "We decided we ought to quit that." Instead, they began purchasing equipment together, splitting purchase price and profits. "There would be some margin that way, and we'd both get something out of it," says Carl.

Remembering his father's advice from the Rexmont store days, Carl knew that you didn't have to buy at the lowest price, or sell at the highest, but in between there was room to make some money.

Another early problem, and one Carl would run up against frequently as he built his business, was a shortage of cash. With his money tied up in farming, he lacked the capital he needed to buy tractors. So after his first few deals, Carl's father agreed to put up the money to buy equipment, and they split profits 50-50.

Carl's parents, John and Bertha, provided financial and moral support as Carl and Margaret built a business and a family. Carl and Margaret are flanked by John and Bertha in this 1950s photo.

"It worked out really well for both of us," says Carl. "When these young fellows would start up farming, my father provided the cattle, and I supplied all of the equipment." The same 12-foot truck hauled both, with the sides coming off to haul tractors and being put back on to haul cows. By 1953, he was hauling enough equipment that he purchased a16-foot truck just for his business. "Then I took the sides off for good," he says.

Though his business was building, it wasn't at all clear that he would be successful. Carl still remembers one Sunday afternoon in those early years, when fellow equipment dealer and family friend Jake Gockley was visiting in Myerstown. "I had maybe four discs, a couple plows, and a couple of pieces down behind the barn," Carl recalls. "And my dad said to Jake, 'Do you think Carl will ever sell all of this stuff?' Today, it wouldn't even be a semi-load full of equipment."

As his appetite for equipment grew, Carl began to cast a wider net, buying from and sometimes partnering with dealers in neighboring counties. In York County he partnered with Guy Rentzel and in Reinholds in Northern Lancaster County, Jake Gockley, referring customers back and forth and purchasing equipment from each other.

"I had a Ford dealer named James Straley over in York County," Carl recalls, "who knew when I was milking cows and he would call at night." They would consummate a deal for two or three tractors, and then the dealer would add one stipulation: "You gotta' have them here by the time we open tomorrow morning." So when the milking was finished, Carl and Margaret would load up the truck with tractors and depart for Dover, York County. Carl would try to catch some winks on the way home while Margaret drove the truck.

Come morning, Carl's dad would help Margaret with the barn work while sleep-deprived Carl, who was out hauling cattle or moving tractors almost every night, had trouble rising. "My dad would come in, and he was disgusted," Carl recalls.

Soon, Carl wasn't finding enough equipment to buy in Eastern Pennsylvania, and he began going out of state. Every other week or so, he ran a regular loop down along the Eastern Shore of Delaware and Maryland, often accompanied by fellow dealer Jake Gockley and his young son, Elmer, who most people know today as "Honey." Young Elmer idolized Carl and looked forward to these regular excursions.

"At that time," explains Elmer, "the dealers were sitting so full of machinery and you could buy more than you ever cared to haul."

They would leave home by 5 a.m. to be in position somewhere beyond Elkton, Maryland, for the opening of the first dealer at 7:30. If they got off to a late start, they ran the risk of getting behind Clyde Keener or Maryland dealer Paul Clay, who traveled the same circuit and would have all the bargains picked out.

From there the trip was carefully choreographed, with one of the longer legs falling over midday, when the dealers were out to lunch. Carl and company didn't take time to stop for lunch at the risk of missing out on a deal down the road. Finally, after 5 p.m. when the dealers were closed and the work was done, Carl would pull into a diner near Chestertown for supper. With full stomachs, and on a good day, a full inventory of purchases, Carl and his cohorts would rehash the deals of the day as they traveled home, arriving back in Myerstown around midnight.

On the off weeks of his Eastern Shore travels, Carl headed west to the bi-weekly Yoder & Frey Consignment Auction near Archbold, Ohio. Located in the northwest corner of Ohio, near the Michigan state line, Archhbold was a 500-mile drive. Carl would work a full day at home on Monday, and leave early evening, driving the first 100 miles alone to the Fort Littleton turnpike interchange. There he would rendezvous with auctioneer friend Ralph Horst, who ran an auction of his own in Marion, Pennsylvania.

Together they would complete the final 400 miles of the journey, arriving in western Ohio after 2 a.m. After catching a few hours of sleep in a hotel, they made their way to the all-day auction, which sometimes continued until midnight on Tuesday. Carl would settle up, see that his purchases were loaded on trucks, and Carl and Ralph would drive home through the night. The last 100 miles, traveling alone, were the toughest, Carl recalls.

He would arrive back home in Myerstown by mid-morning on Wednesday, tired and cranky, but there was no time for rest. He had just purchased perhaps 30 or 40 pieces of equipment that needed to be sold. "I would call and tell Margaret that I am home and back at work," he recalls, "and I would finish out the day."

Twice a month for close to two decades Carl would complete this grueling routine. "By the time I got home and rested up," he says, "it was time to go again."

Things would improve somewhat in the mid-1960s, when eldest son Lloyd was old enough to drive, while Carl slept in the backseat. But those days were still far off.

The Kids or the Cows

Back at the farm, Carl's growing equipment business was starting to impact other areas of life. The farmhouse dining room was pressed into service as an office, with a sofa in the kitchen serving as a makeshift waiting area. The kitchen waiting room made sense, because Margaret often ended up feeding out-of-town customers, anyway.

When Carl was on the road at sales and equipment dealers, he communicated with the home "office" via a two-way radio, whose base station occupied the dining room. The three-car garage across Race Street from the house became the shop. The field behind the barn evolved into a salvage yard.

But the house that doubled as an office also was home to a rapidly growing family. In the early years of their marriage, Carl and Margaret could get away with working day and night. They

Expensive Feed

Though they didn't have a lot of money to spare at times in the early years of their marriage, one time Carl and Margaret fed their cows some very expensive feed. In those days, they ground their own feed with a hammer mill that blew the feed up into a mixer. One day Carl was up tinkering with the mixer, when Margaret came out to ask him for a few dollars to pay for some baked goods. The tenants who rented the other half of the farmhouse had just paid their rent, so Carl was flush with cash. He tossed his wallet down to Margaret. She took what she needed and, since Carl wasn't easily accessible, she carelessly laid the bulging wallet on the hammer mill for him to retrieve when he climbed down. In the meantime, Carl solved the problem with the mixer and his dad cranked up the mill to grind some feed. "When we started up the hammer mill," says Carl, "it chopped and blew my wallet. We fed $20 bills to the cows."

would milk till 6:00 or 7:00 p.m., and then Carl would go haul cattle and equipment.

"Half the time we didn't eat," Margaret recalls, "or we ate at 10:00 at night and then we went to bed." With Margaret tied up at the barn and Carl on the road, there just wasn't time for regular family dinners.

Another common supper plan was a soup and sandwich at Mary Elton's barbeque restaurant along Route 422 east of town, where Country Fare Restaurant is located today. But sometimes there wasn't even time for that.

"I remember a couple times," says Margaret, "where we ate a dish of ice cream and went to bed."

When they did have time to eat, they didn't always have groceries. Margaret recalls one time in their early years when they had to borrow grocery money from Carl's parents to hold them over until the next milk check. Other times they took eggs to the grocer to trade for groceries.

"We weren't poor people," Carl offers.

"No, we were dumb!" says Margaret with a laugh.

Saturday night Hershey Bears hockey games were their one regular respite from work. Carl and Margaret were season ticket holders for a number of years.

But as the business and family grew, the stress of managing farm and family was no laughing matter. By the mid-1950s Carl was at an auction somewhere just about every day. "He was building a business and I was home taking care of all these children," explains Margaret. Some weeks Margaret would pack Carl's bag Monday morning and he would head out-of-state to equipment auctions, not to return until the following weekend. "He'd go out to Ohio and the Midwest," she says, "come back, and the next week we'd start over."

One Decision Carl Never Made

Carl Wenger has made a lot of big decisions in his life, some with thousands of dollars at stake. But one decision he never made was what clothes he would wear. Up until the time he married, his mother always laid out his clothes for him in the morning and packed his bags for trips. When he married Margaret, she picked up where Bertha left off, laying out pants, shirt, and undergarments each day he was home, and carefully packing his bags for each trip. The only dress decisions for Carl to make were whether to add a bolo tie and which Western hat to wear.

Meanwhile, Margaret struggled to keep up with everything at home. "It was a lot of work," she laments. "And when I was milking cows I would often go and milk by myself. His dad would come and feed the cows. Carl would call home from out of town somewhere at an auction and say he was running late and he wouldn't be home or whatever. I would get the cows in and milk."

By fall 1955 Margaret had four little children, along with 42 cows, making demands on her time, and a husband who was on the road day and night. Carl's mother, Bertha, helped frequently with the children so Margaret could work, and the Wengers did hire a hand to help with the barn work. But Margaret was still overloaded. By the late 1950s something had to give.

"I remember telling Carl that I could not do it anymore," says Margaret. "Either you get rid of the cows or get rid of the kids."

They decided to keep the kids and relieve Margaret of milking duties. Eventually they would phase out the dairy business, entirely, but not before older sons Lloyd and Larry would get a taste of milking cows, themselves.

6

Wenger's Farm Machinery, Inc.

By the late 1950s, it was clear that Carl's future lay more in farm equipment than in farming. Faced with an unsustainable workload, especially for Margaret, they began phasing out the dairy operation and moved toward formalizing the business.

In 1958 Carl and his father merged the equipment business, which Carl owned, with the farm and cattle dealership, which John owned, and incorporated as Wenger's Farm Machinery. John received three-fifths of the stock and Carl two-fifths but,

Carl and his father incorporated Wenger's Farm Machinery in 1958. This Myerstown Merchandiser ad dates from around that time.

since Carl was running the business, he received two dollars from the profit for every dollar his father received.

"That sounded good and fair," says Carl. "But the kind of operator I was, I didn't take anything out; I just kept building and building. So everything that I was building was three-fifths on his side and two-fifths on my side, and I was doing the work."

To remedy the situation, John agreed that "to level things out" they would take a bonus at the end of the year and Carl would get the stock for the bonus. "That sounded real good," says Carl. But when tax time came, Carl had to borrow $20,000 to pay his taxes because of the additional income. Eventually they worked it out so that Carl's portion of the business grew to equal his father's.

An Appreciation for Fine Cars

While most of his profits were getting poured back into the business, Carl was making enough money that in 1958 he decided to indulge his taste for fine cars. From the time he had climbed behind the wheel of the '49 Oldsmobile that his dad bought for him as a teen, Carl always had an appreciation for nice cars. During the 1950s he drove Buicks, each one remembered by family friend Elmer Gockley, who ticks off the models and features of Carl's cars like they were his own.

There was the '52 two-tone green four-door sedan, followed by a '54 mint green and white two-door hardtop. Then came the '56 four-door pink and white hardtop. Carl didn't sit good in that one, so he replaced it the following year with a spacious '57 Roadmaster 75. While a new Buick every year or two was nice, what Carl really had his heart set on was a Cadillac. But he wasn't sure how his father would feel about such an indulgence.

When Carl broached the topic, he was surprised at his father's take on it. "Dad said, 'Hey, as hard as you're working, if you want that car you're entitled to it,'" Carl remembers. "That's all that my dad said. I thought he might jerk a little bit, but he said the other way." (Eventually Carl would keep his dad in Cadillacs, as well, but John would accept a new one only when Carl could convince him that he needed a tax deduction for the business.)

So late in 1958 Carl purchased a lightly used '58 teal Cadillac at Hammond Cadillac in Milford, Delaware, the first of many that he would purchase from the dealership.

Two years later Elmer Gockley was along with Carl on an equipment-purchasing trip in Delaware, when Carl traded in the '58 for his first *new* Cadillac, a gray 1960 model. On the way home, Carl handed the keys to Elmer. "He left me drive it," Elmer recalls, still with wonder in his voice 50 years later. "I mean, he was my hero!"

Carl doesn't remember how many different Cadillacs he has owned, and he regrets that he didn't take pictures of them. Eventually he settled into the pattern of trading up for a new one every year or so.

For a time it was baler twine that kept Carl and Margaret in new cars. Margaret would oversee sales of baler twine throughout the year. While the profit margin wasn't large, they would sell enough volume and use the profits to upgrade to a new Caddy.

One year, Carl cut down on his "out money" on a new car by dealing in tires. He had noticed that the dealer in Delaware always put new tires on trade-ins before reselling. So he inquired what those tires cost. He learned he could get a better price at Bamberger's in Lebanon. So when it came time to trade up on his next Cadillac, he filled his used one with tires he purchased from Bambergers and traded the old car filled with new tires even up for a new car.

While the upgrade still cost him some, Carl did make a profit on the tires and got to enjoy the art of the deal. "He needed tires," Carl summarizes. "I said, 'If you're going to be buying tires, you might as well be buying them off of me.'"

In June 1962 Carl made what could be considered another luxury purchase, when he obtained a cabin on nine acres of land on the Blue Mountain in nearby Berks County. Carl wasn't the type to while away his weekends up on the mountain, but he liked the cabin and thought it would be a good investment. Through the years since then, many others have enjoyed the magnificent view from the cabin, including the Myerstown Lions, who held an annual "Steak Night" there, and the state FFA officers, who held their annual retreat at the cabin for many years, beginning when Glenn was a state officer in the early 1980s.

Building for Growth

By the early 1960s Carl had a sizable and growing business, but didn't have facilities to match. He still was working out of his home, garage, and fields. Other than the machinery parked and piled around the farm buildings, the main marker of the

The construction of a separate building to house the business in 1964 was a major improvement. The building is pictured here around 1970, after some improvements to the front of the building had been added.

business was a sign hanging at the corner of the driveway that read, "New, Used & Abused Tractors & Farm Machinery."

Longtime friend and neighbor George Swanger, who was born in 1950, played with the Wenger children, and found odd jobs to do around the Wenger farm and shop, recalls, "The Wenger garage was always full of tractors in various states of repair. Some tractors had the rear ends supported by blocks. Others were completely in half, while an engine was being installed. It was organized chaos, but all part of the business plan."

The parts business, which today is housed in a state-of-the-art facility with computerized, online inventory, was somewhat less organized. When a customer would call for a part, Carl would send Harry Stohler out to the salvage lot to pull the piece off of the appropriate tractor.

Things took a major step forward in 1964 with the construction of a separate building to house the business. Located at 251 South Race Street, across the street and north of the farmhouse, the new building was a huge improvement over the makeshift dining room office and shop in the garage.

Carl struck a deal with a contractor friend, agreed on plans, and then essentially ignored the project during the months of construction. "I was so busy selling equipment that I didn't go to that building more than a few times while it was being built," he recalls. As a result of staying focused on selling, by the time the building was complete Carl had made enough money to pay for it.

Elmer Gockley remembers his first impression of the new building: "I thought, gosh, why's a man putting up such a big building, this enormous building with all this loading dock around it." But he soon realized that, "It wasn't more than enough. It was too small already."

Over time, Carl would add a paint shop, an oil room, and a sales room. The block building would serve well for more than three decades, when the business would relocate to a huge

The Wisdom of Carl

One time Carl's singular focus on selling got him in trouble with a pair of customers. It wasn't quite the wisdom of Solomon, but like the Old Testament King, Carl had to resolve a situation where two people lay claim to one item that couldn't easily be divided. Instead of a baby, it was a John Deere tractor. Carl had advertised the tractor at a bargain price. Customers were lined up to see him on a hectic day, but when a friend came into the store, Carl welcomed him into his office ahead of some others. In the course of the conversation, Carl sold his friend the tractor. A man who had been patiently waiting came into the office next and said he wanted to buy the tractor that Carl had just sold. Carl was in a bind.

He recognized that the second man should have had first crack at the tractor, but he had already sold it. To resolve the issue, Carl called in both men, took responsibility, and apologized for his error. Then he proposed they resolve the issue with an impromptu auction. The winning bidder would take home the tractor for the advertised price. But he also would pay the losing bidder the difference between the advertised price and the winning bid. Carl's friend ended up paying a little more than he had anticipated for the tractor, and the other man went home with some money to compensate him for his loss. While the losing bidder still went away grumbling, Carl had done the best he could. "I walked away from it," says Carl, "feeling I had been fair after I made the initial mistake."

modern facility along Route 501 that Elmer Gockley—or anyone else—could never have imagined back in 1964. The original
building continues to serve as the Wengers of Myerstown machine shop today.

Expanding the Family

By the time the new building was constructed to house
the expanding business, Carl and Margaret also had expanded
their family considerably. The three younger children—David,

*By 1966, when this photo was taken, Carl and Margaret's family had
grown to include seven children. Pictured (clockwise from back left) are
Lloyd, Larry, Carol, Davey, Rose, Nancy, and Glenn.*

Glenn, and Rose—were born in 1960, 1962, and 1963, respec-tively, for a total of seven kids age 12 and younger.

Margaret remembers her sister visiting during these years and marveling that one woman could do all that Margaret did. Margaret explained to her, "Hey, you go to the hospital, you have a baby, you bring it home, and it blends in with all the rest of them. You do what you have to do."

While Carl was good to his children, says Margaret, the day-to-day care of the kids fell entirely to her. Without a hint of resentment in her voice, she observes that she can't recall Carl ever changing a diaper, babysitting, or signing a school form for any of the seven children. He was focused on the business.

Even most holidays Carl was away. There were big auctions somewhere in the country on New Year's Day, Memorial Day, July 4, even Thanksgiving. On Thanksgiving, Margaret recalls, "He would come home for dinner and then he was off again at an auction somewhere."

The one exception was Christmas, when the family was able to enjoy a day together at home.

Not only did Carl work on holidays, but family vacations weren't something the Wengers considered. "We worked all the time," says Margaret. "We never took the family and went on vacation. Where do you go with seven children, you know? We couldn't even all get in the same vehicle."

When the family did go for a drive, they often were bathed in the smoke of Carl's White Owl or Dutch Masters cigars. "He was heavy on cigars," says Lloyd. The older children endured many a trip in a smoke-filled Oldsmobile, some in the dead of winter with windows rolled up tight.

Larry remembers a business trip to Tarboro, North Carolina, some years later that he went on with Carl, Lloyd, and two business associates, all of whom were smokers. Larry was not. "Guess where I got to sit?" Larry deadpans. "I was in the back seat on the hump, so I couldn't even open the window. All four of them smoked 12 hours on the way to Tarboro and 12 hours back."

The size of their family also limited meal invitations in the homes of others. Few people were eager to set nine extra places at the table to accommodate the Wenger family. One place they did visit regularly on Sunday afternoons was the Jake Gockley home, near Reinholds, in northern Lancaster County. Jake and Carl had two things in common—both were used farm equipment dealers and both had large families. While Carl and Jake talked tractors, the Gockley and Wenger children enjoyed playing together on summer afternoons.

Even when Carl was home, he wasn't always emotionally available to his children. He would arrive home after a week of travel, leave the children with a sitter, and take Margaret out Saturday evening. Then, starved for sleep, Carl would spend Sunday afternoons napping. When the family had a Sunday cookout at their cabin or another family event, Carl nearly always slipped upstairs to sleep away much of the afternoon.

"Some of those years when he was on the road," says Larry, "that's when he would catch up on his rest. He would come home maybe late Saturday or Sunday morning and he would rest Sunday."

The older children recall that, for a period of time when Carl was working day and night to build his business, their grandparents made sure the children got to church. But Davey, one of the younger three children, says that by the time he was on the scene, Carl attended church faithfully with his family—although it often took a well-placed elbow from Margaret during the sermon to prevent Carl from beginning his afternoon nap early.

As their family continued to grow, Margaret worked hard to keep them all fed. "Carl's mother and I had a big garden and I would do a lot of canning and freezing and meal planning," she recalls. "It was a lot when you had nine people come to the table three times a day."

For a time, Margaret baked and the family consumed a nine-by-thirteen-inch cake each day. Arriving home from school hungry, the kids would devour a piece of cake. Cake was then served as dessert at supper. And if any was left, it was polished off with glasses of milk before bedtime. "The next day you started all over again," Margaret reminisces.

Margaret and her children have many fond memories of those years when the children were growing up, and all seem grateful for the family business that Carl worked so hard to build, ultimately for their benefit. But sometimes his children—especially his daughters who would have fewer opportunities

Dealing for Dining

Margaret didn't always have to cook, thanks to some dealing for dining that Carl did. Twice he successfully swapped equipment for fine dining. During the early 1960s Carl stopped in at a new restaurant in the woods near Akron, in Lancaster County. Carl liked the food and got to talking with the owner. "He needed a chain saw to clean up the woods and, like me, he had all of his money tied up in his business," says Carl. "So I made a deal with him. I sold him a chain saw and took it out as a credit for restaurant charges." The restaurant was the Log Cabin.

He closed a similar deal with John Brody, owner of the Timbers restaurant in Mt. Gretna. John had a mile-long lane to his restaurant, with no way to plow it. Each fall, for a time, Carl parked a tractor with chains and blade at the Timbers, and collected a monthly rental fee in restaurant charges. The deal satisfied Carl's appetite for good food and John's need for a snow plow.

to interact with their father through business and FFA involve-ments—yearned for a closer relationship with their dad.

Concerned at one point that Carl was missing out on his chil-dren's lives, Margaret warned Carl, "One day they're going to go out that front door and you won't know what happened to them." While Margaret was correct that Carl missed a lot of family life, her assessment of what would happen to the children when they left the house turned out to be wrong. Looking back, she observes, "All seven of them walked out my front door and right into his."

Beginnings of a Family Business

In fact, while the younger children were joining the family in the early 1960s, the older ones already were joining the family business. Just as Carl's parents had given him age-appropriate responsibilities from little on up, Carl also gave his children the responsibility they deserved at an early age.

He assigned farm chores and found small tasks they could do in the shop and office, such as emptying waste cans, and picking up nails and screws from the parking lot so that customers' tires wouldn't get punctured. As the kids grew older and asked for bicycles, and later motorcycles and cars, Carl would say they could have whatever they wanted, but they had to earn it.

While Carl was largely absent from home life, as his children grew older, he was able to build bonds by incorporating them into the business—especially his sons. As was true of their fa-ther, hard work would become a way of life for Carl's sons and daughters, but such an upbringing involved tradeoffs.

"We didn't do some of the normal things that other families did," explains Larry. "I didn't go hunting or fishing. None of us really got involved in sports. We were all busy working on the farm at home."

Although Margaret had been relieved of milking duties some years earlier, Carl and his father maintained a milking herd into Lloyd and Larry's high school days in the late 1960s.

"I remember getting up at 5 o'clock in the morning before school," says Larry. "Lloyd and I would go down and milk the cows before we went to school. We'd come back into the house and change, and go to school, and come home from school and go milk cows again."

"And then you would have that smell with you," adds Lloyd. "You almost were ashamed to go to school because you smelled like a farmer."

Lloyd continues, "I went to Grandpa one day and I said, 'Grandpa, we cannot keep doing this. You're running us ragged.' We were getting tired of getting kicked against the wall." (Many in the herd were first-calf heifers, who didn't appreciate being milked.) John began gradually to sell off his herd and the boys were finally freed from milking duties.

The Wengers' experience with roller skates further illustrates how they were a little different than most families. Many kids have a pair of skates to play with. The Wenger children had hundreds of pairs to work on and sell for a profit.

It happened around 1960. In addition to owning some farms, a regular customer of Carl's also owned a roller rink, north of the State Farm Show Complex at Harrisburg. The rink was going out of business. Carl decided to attend the public sale to see what they had. When it came time to sell the skates, the auctioneer had trouble attracting bids on individual pairs. He tried selling them by the dozen, but fared no better. Finally, he put hundreds of pairs of the black skates up for sale, all for one bid.

Carl brought them home in 55-gallon drums and put the older children to work organizing and fixing them up for resale. Wenger's Farm Machinery had branched out into roller skate sales.

Always on the lookout for opportunities to make a few dollars, Wenger's later would dabble in shoes and bicycles, and barter tractors for services. Other deals involved golf carts, paddle boats, an old fire engine, turn-of-the-century antique thrashers, and even a replica of the General Lee car made famous on the Dukes of Hazzard television show.

"Child Labor"

With his growing child labor force, Carl found other ways to involve his kids in the business. A frequent problem he ran into was that on any given Saturday there were more farm sales than he could possibly attend. But with children to do his bidding for him, Carl could cover more than one sale at a time. Beginning with Lloyd, and eventually adding other children as they came of age, Carl would map out his sale schedule for the day, dropping off sons and occasionally daughters at individual sales with instructions on how high to bid on each piece of equipment. Carl would go to the farthest sale, and at the end of the day retrace the route to retrieve kids and equipment.

Lloyd remembers writing the bids his dad quoted him on his hand. "But I soon figured out after a couple sales when it rained, that didn't work too well." He switched to index cards instead. But that still didn't solve all of his problems. At one sale the auctioneer sold the row of equipment in reverse order from Lloyd's cards, causing confusion.

At another sale, the auctioneer refused to take 12-year-old Lloyd's bid on a piece of equipment worth thousands of dollars. So from then on, Carl would explain the situation to the auctioneer before leaving Lloyd behind. Sometimes an auctioneer would playfully coax Lloyd to check his card again to see if his pop didn't want him to pay more. "He'd kind of harass me a little bit," Lloyd recalls.

A Shoestring Operation

While Wenger's mostly made its money by buying and selling, some of the more memorable deals involved bartering, like the time in the late 1970s when Lloyd traded a combine for a semi-truckload of shoes. A customer from the Hanover area was interested in a Case combine, and also wanted to get out of the shoe business. Seeing an opportunity to turn a profit, Lloyd put his best foot forward and traded the combine for the shoe inventory, no strings attached.

But the deal got off on the wrong foot when Davey and other employees were sent to pick up the shoes. Unbeknownst to Lloyd, the store displayed one shoe from each pair and kept the other in the back. Nothing was matched. The guys simply gathered everything up, threw some 10,000 pairs of shoes into big boxes and loaded them up. By the time the footwear made it to Myerstown, there were somewhat fewer than 10,000 pairs, since some had tumbled off the open flatbed truck. "Davey heard on the CB (radio) that there were shoes on the highway," Carl recalls, "so he took the truck and hid for a little while because he didn't want to go back and pick up all of those shoes."

Many of the shoes that made it the whole way were, to put it politely, unattractive. "Oh, they were ugly," laments youngest daughter, Rose, who as a little girl already had enough fashion sense to recognize ugly. "It was embarrassing."

When the shoes arrived at the store, they were dumped out on piles in the large combine building and the kids began the hopeless task of finding matching pairs. They found a few, put them on shelves, and ran ads in the paper. But when customers saw a style they liked and asked for it in a different size, the Wengers couldn't deliver.

So they scrounged big boxes from a nearby appliance store, filled them with shoes, and let customers rummage through the piles themselves. The lucky customer who found a match could get a pair of decent shoes for a buck. Or he or she could pay $250 for a big boxful, which attracted some flea market dealers. The final 16 boxes were bought by a local businessman, who donated them to an overseas mission, says Lloyd. In the end, the Wengers were relieved to be out of the shoe business and refocused their attention on farm equipment.

And the system didn't always go like clockwork. Lloyd remembers waiting . . . a lot. "If he got tied up a long time where he was—which he was good at doing—you know talking to people and stuff," says Lloyd, "we'd end up sitting on porches, waiting for him to come back and pick us up."

One Saturday Carl dropped Lloyd off at a small sale in Central New Jersey, with instructions to buy a John Deere 630. The larger sale that Carl was attending was further north and lasted longer than he had expected. He returned late in the day to find Lloyd sitting on the porch, where he had been perched for three or four hours, waiting.

"Everybody left," says Lloyd. "The stuff was all gone, the auctioneer left." But Lloyd got the tractor—the most expensive item sold that day.

For the most part the system worked, helping to build the business and educating Lloyd, Larry, David, and Glenn, especially, in the value of tractors and equipment.

But even with a large family, Carl didn't have enough kids to cover all the sales. On Saturdays when he had more sales than available kids, he enlisted local farmers to do his bidding. And he continued to expand his range of out-of-state travel.

Becoming a National Dealer

Through contacts in Archbold, Ohio, Carl was led to Stahl Brothers Auction in Fletcher, Ohio, and then to a regular auction in Stilesville, Indiana, some 620 miles from Myerstown. Next he found his way to an auction in Carson, Iowa, and then Cornlea, Nebraska. Then he began discovering sales in the South, first in Charlotte, North Carolina, then in Georgia, Florida, and Alabama. By this time, Carl was beginning to fly to auctions to save time. Longtime friend Clyde Deck, who owned a Seneca twin engine airplane, began flying Carl to equipment sales, the beginnings of Clyde's charter flight business and the privately owned Deck Airport in Myerstown.

Decked out in his Western hat and wearing his big belt buckle emblazoned with the Wenger "W," Carl became an easily recognizable figure at auctions across the United States. "I can walk into an auction around the country," says Carl, "and the auctioneer will stop while he is selling a piece and welcome me there."

As Carl became more of a national dealer, he was able to exploit regional differences in equipment needs and prices. For a time, Allis Chalmers round balers were available in the east, but were in demand farther west. Later, when Eastern Shore farmers converted from pull-type combines to self-propelled combines, Carl scooped up all the pull-behind models he could and sold them in Myerstown, where they still were being used on smaller farms.

One year in the late 1960s, a cornpicker glut in the west led to brisk sales for Carl in the east. "We had a couple years of drought around here," Carl recalls, "and nobody was buying any pickers." When eastern farmers were blessed the following year with a bumper crop, they suddenly needed cornpickers. In the west, however, farmers were moving from tractor-mounted pickers to combines with corn heads, so demand for cornpickers bottomed out.

Clyde Deck flew Carl to auctions in early years, helping to expand Carl's reach and launch Clyde's charter flight business. Clyde and Carl are pictured here at the Deck Airport in Myerstown in 1996.

Carl bought pickers in the west and sold them in the east, moving 109 in 90 days. At auction in Archbold, Ohio, he bought a whole row of cornpickers. The good ones he could resell, and from the others he could profit by salvaging the mounting kits needed to attach the pickers to the tractors. Demand was so urgent that he couldn't take time to send his trucks out from Pennsylvania, but instead hired local trucks to haul the equipment home.

"I hauled pickers and I hauled pickers," he says. "I'd get home here and they'd be waiting in line when the truck got here so that they could get choice off of the truck. I remember we'd load them off onto the dock and by the time we were unloaded we would be loading them up again on somebody else's truck."

"It just so happened that needing them here and an excess inventory out there was right at the same time," Carl explains. "Out there nobody wanted them. It was up to me. And I'd step in and do it. I had guts."

Of course, the trick to success is recognizing when to stop buying. "It doesn't stay good forever," Carl explains. "You get a good shot like that and then it is all over."

Evidently, Carl was better than most at recognizing trends. Many others tried to make it in the equipment business, but ultimately failed. Carl's business continued to grow as he bought out the inventories of other dealers. "We had guys start up and they couldn't make it," says Carl. "And we went and bought them out, just went and bought their whole inventory. It looked easy to other people who tried it, but they found out it wasn't as easy as they thought."

During the 1960s Carl sold hundreds of Allis Chalmers round balers like the ones on the truck in this photo. As he became a national dealer, Carl learned to profit from regional equipment trends.

Children of the Board

By the mid-1960s, Carl's business was flourishing, but Carl was concerned. Sharing ownership with his aging father, Carl worried that if anything happened to John, Carl would have to pay for the business all over again through taxes. And he was even more concerned that if anything happened to him in his travels, Margaret and the children might not be able to afford the taxes to keep the business.

With these transition issues troubling him, Carl received a visit one day in fall 1967 from Al Hicks, a representative of the Philadelphia Life Insurance Company and one of Carl's trusted advisors. Noticing Carl's vacant stare out the window toward his father's home, Al inquired what had Carl feeling down. Carl told him: "You know, I'm here working my tail off and my dad's up there—and he was up in age—and if anything happens to him I can't even keep my business because he owns half of it."

Carrying this growing burden, Carl hadn't found a way to talk to his dad about it. Al encouraged Carl to get on the phone to set up a time to talk. Carl called his dad and, though it was suppertime, John was ready to talk. So they immediately went to discuss their relationship and the future of the business. As it turned out, his dad had been pondering some of the same issues that were troubling Carl.

Al explained to John the potential negative tax implications if anything happened to either partner and they discussed how to transition the business. A week later, John had compiled two lists—one of considerable assets he wanted to get rid of, and a much smaller one of things he wanted to keep. "His assets were a lot to get rid of at one time," says Carl. "The part he wanted to get rid of was a big deal."

So Carl, Al Hicks, and financial advisor John Good looked at how to make the transition without accruing "an enormous tax bill." John wanted to sell it all to Carl, but Carl didn't want it. "I was flying all over the country," explains Carl, "and I knew if I owned all of it and anything happened to me, my kids could never get it because they couldn't afford the tax on it. They'd have to pay the tax in order to keep it and that would default the operation."

Carl's idea was to sell John's half of the business to the seven children, but John thought it unwise to have such young children as business owners. He finally agreed to split it nine ways, with a share for each child and one each for Carl and Margaret. The transaction was finalized on November 28, 1967.

As a result, all of the children now had an ownership stake in the business, including the two youngest children, who had yet to enter school. Not many children in kindergarten own a business, but such was the case with the youngest Wengers. Since the children were still so young, the company was structured with voting stock for Carl and Margaret and non-voting for the kids. Sometime later, when "all of the kids had their feet flat on the ground" all the stock was converted to voting stock.

To help lower John's tax burden, Carl traded his father some uncollectable accounts for some good assets, which lowered the value of John's estate. John then was able to work at collecting on some of these unpaid accounts. Shares also were transferred over a period of years to the children for the same reasons.

The business had cleared a major hurdle and completed a transition that Carl believed put them on solid footing for the future. While his children had been involved in the business from an early age, now Wenger's officially was a family-owned business, with Carl, Margaret, and the children as its stockholders.

Youngest son Glenn remembers the family holding annual shareholder meetings with the accountant to discuss the state of the business. One of the children who had become a stockholder before he could read, Glenn was on the payroll by age seven, earning five dollars a week to empty waste cans, sweep floors, clean up the salvage yard, and perform other age-appropriate jobs. He was driving tractor and moving equipment

Carl's parents (top) transferred their share of the business to Carl, Margaret, and the seven children in 1967. From that point forward, Carl likes to say, he was working for his children.

by age nine. By the time he was 10, says Glenn, he was posing questions to the accountant at shareholder meetings.

"Business fascinated me and it just came natural to me," says Glenn. "I think it's just a gift that I was given." Except for a brief period when he toyed with enlisting in the Marines, from his early childhood on, Glenn never considered doing anything but following his father's footsteps into the family business.

Carl reflects that as his children grew and took on larger roles in the business, onlookers would ask him how he got all of his kids to stay and work for him. "I would say, 'Hey, they're not working for me. I'm here working for them,'" explains Carl. "And it was the truth. They all owned one ninth of one half of it. And that's what kept the interest of the kids."

As the children married during the 1970s, sons- and daughters-in-law also were incorporated into the business, although Carl admits that he made some mistakes in trying to "Wengerize" new members of the expanding family. Not fully comprehending how much of a headstart his own children had by virtue of growing up in the business, Carl can see now that he initially expected too much of his new family members when they came on board. But over time they would find their niche in the family business and be instrumental in its success.

Though he had cashed out his part of the business, John remained a fixture around Wenger's nearly until his death in 1978. Until diabetes claimed one of his legs, John liked to sit on rolls of baler twine inside the store entrance with a Coke and a chaw of Mail Pouch tobacco and greet customers as they came and went.

His legacy as a savvy entrepreneur and businessman lived on in Carl, and would continue into the next generations. Carl's mother would outlive her husband by 16 years, passing away in 1994. Carl owed much of his business success to his parents, who raised him in a store, modeled hard work, entrusted him with responsibility at a young age, allowed him to make mistakes, and provided capital and counsel as he grew his own business.

Beauty in the Eye of the Beholder

During the 1960s and 1970s, things were going well for Wenger's Farm Machinery, but not everybody appreciated Carl's expanding business. An anonymous writer crafted a letter to the editor of the *Lebanon Daily News* (May 22, 1965, p. 4), lamenting all the rusty equipment that the writer felt was destroying the view and lowering property values of the "lovely homes" in Carl's corner of Myerstown. "These houses face a sea of old and rusted farm implements," the letter noted, "many unusable or unsellable." It concluded, "What a shame to destroy such a lovely view."

By the early 1970s, when this aerial photo was taken, Carl had built a sprawling business at the intersection of Race and Park Streets.

But beauty is in the eye of the beholder, and Carl could appreciate those rusted farm implements in ways that some of his neighbors could not.

7

Incorporating the Next Generation

The 1970s brought explosive growth to Wenger's Farm Machinery, with annual revenue reaching nearly $5 million by mid-decade. As the business grew, so did the responsibilities of Carl's children, as he continued to incorporate them into the business. During the 1970s the older sons began taking on larger roles. As soon as he turned 16 in November 1967, Lloyd began purchasing at auctions on his own. "(Dad) wouldn't even go to the sale," Lloyd explains. "We'd go over the list in the paper. He would say, 'If you like it, pay this amount. If you don't like it, pay this amount.'"

Lloyd also became Carl's chauffeur on long trips to out-of-state auctions, driving 500 miles at night so Carl could sleep. The novelty of driving wore off quickly on these grueling trips, but it became more bearable for Lloyd when the auction at Archbold began paying him to drive tractors across the auction block while his dad was doing the bidding.

When Lloyd was named FFA Eastern Region Star Agri-Businessman in 1971, a local news reporter documented Lloyd's growing role in the business: "Wenger (Lloyd) began working for Wenger's Farm Machinery, Inc., as a mechanic's aide when he was 10. Last year, 19-year-old Wenger sold nearly half a million dollars worth of farm machinery, making him one of the top salesmen of agricultural machinery in Pennsylvania."

The Biggest Deal

Carl's son Lloyd earned his biggest commission when he was still shy of his 25th birthday. He became aware of some cornheads—attachments to put on combines to harvest corn—at Long Manufacturing in North Carolina, a dealer that specialized in irregular equipment manufactured in Romania. The pieces were blue, but had John Deere parts numbers on them. The price was right.

"At that time cornheads were really hot," Lloyd recalls. "Dad and I flew down to Long's and met with Bill Long, himself. We bought every cornhead he had. It was trailer truckloads and trailer truckloads. We paid like $75,000 for the whole works."

Lloyd came home and called two equipment dealers from the Midwest. "Both customers knew that I had them and both customers wanted them," Lloyd recounts. A dealer from Minnesota immediately boarded a plane for Myerstown. Carl vacated his office so Lloyd could meet privately with the customer.

After some small talk, the buyer placed a $250,000 check on the desk in front of wide-eyed Lloyd. Lloyd breathlessly rushed out to his dad to ask what he should do. Carl replied that Lloyd was old enough to handle it himself and told him, "Go, do whatever you need to do."

Lloyd sealed the deal. In less than a week he had turned over the cornheads for a 300 percent profit. "I walked out of there with a quarter of a million dollar check in my hand," Lloyd recalls, still with wonder in his voice three decades later. "I was shaking in my boots when I had that check in my hand."

With the business buoyed by the big deal, brothers Davey and Larry recall that they immediately spent some of the profit on junker cars to participate in a local demolition derby. The only downside was that Lloyd's commission was so big that his dad decided to stretch out the payment over the better part of a year.

To motivate his son, Carl paid Lloyd on commission. "I never ever got a salary," Lloyd recalls. "Dad always wanted me on commission. He said if you're on commission, you work harder, you earn more, you really set your own pay schedule."

In addition to selling equipment, Lloyd and his new bride, Kitty, operated a 60-acre farm at the time.

After a stint in the Navy, Larry returned to the business in 1974, and by then Nancy and Carol, both in their early 20s, helped out regularly in the office. Davey, Glenn, and Rose, still young teens, continued to grow in involvement in the business, which by then was branching out beyond farm equipment.

Dabbling in Dozers

In addition to strong demand for used farm equipment and tractors, the business also grew by adding construction equipment sales. Carl began dabbling in dozers during the 1960s, with the help of early employee Curtis Bashore. "We had some calls for small crawlers," Carl recalls. "I didn't understand crawlers, but Curtis did."

Curtis first purchased three crawlers (bulldozers) from Vilsmeier Equipment, located along Route 309, north of Philadelphia, at Montgomeryville. Clyde Keener in Manheim became another source. Some of the crawlers and other construction equipment were used on area farms, but Carl also supplied equipment for some new businesses that were just getting off of the ground—or in some cases into the ground.

When Galen Wolgemuth started a landfill and trash hauling business near Schaefferstown, Carl remembers selling him his first truck and first crawler. The Studebaker with a dump box served as a garbage truck, and the Cletrac dozer worked in the landfill.

Carl sold a dozer to John Gingrich, who during the 1960s dug the ponds for the Limestone Springs Fish Hatchery in

Millardsville. "I had an International TD6 that needed some work," Carl explains. John spent many hours in the cold in Carl's field fixing the piece up over the winter, and was ready to dig when spring arrived.

Carl sold his first backhoe, an 8N Ford tractor-loader-backhoe that he picked up from a dealer in Mountville, to Lloyd Hower for his fledgling trash hauling business, which today is known as TNT Sanitation. With the profit from the backhoe sale, Carl visited furniture dealer "Pinky" Leininger and purchased the first color television that was sold in Myerstown.

When operators of coal fields to the north of Myerstown began to buy their crawlers from Wenger's, the construction portion of the business took off. During the 1980s, salvaged construction equipment parts would become another important part of the business.

Auctions of His Own

While Carl continued to travel extensively to auctions around the country, by the early 1970s he regularly was hosting auctions of his own at Race Street. He had begun holding annual spring auctions in the mid-1950s and added regular fall sales in the 1960s, utilizing mostly local auctioneers. He held auctions inside, outside, even at night under the lights, and most were very profitable.

He remembers one sale that was less successful because of a scheduling oversight. "I scheduled an auction on Ascension Day," he recalls, "and automatically eliminated attendance by all of our Amish and Mennonite customers." While the holiday commemorating Christ's ascension to heaven takes a backseat to Memorial Day in the mainstream American culture, the Plain community wouldn't conduct business on the Christian holiday. "It was a very big mistake," says Carl.

First Annual

FALL CONSIGNMENT & INVENTORY REDUCTION SALE
TUESDAY, SEPTEMBER 19th
STARTING AT 10:30 A. M.

CORN HARVESTING EQUIPMENT

All Kinds Of Tractor And Horse Drawn Machinery

BACKHOE OUTFIT - BALERS - PLOWS - COMBINES

HARVESTERS - ELEVATORS

DISC and SPRING HARROWS - RAKES - GRAIN DRILL

CORN PLANTERS - HARDWARE - TOOLS

Lots Of Machinery Not Listed.
If You Have Any Surplus Machinery To Sell,
Bring It In For The Sale.

AUCTIONEERS

Ralph Horst And Russell Kehr

Lunch By: Group #2 Farm Women.

We Sell On Commission
PRIVATE SALES DAILY

Wenger's Farm Machinery

SOUTH RACE STREET, MYERSTOWN, LEBANON COUNTY, PA.
BETWEEN READING AND LEBANON
PHONE: 866-2138

Carl began holding his own equipment auctions in the 1950s, and held them more frequently by the 1970s. This sale bill is from the first annual fall auction, held early in the 1960s.

A January 18-19, 1974, auction fared better. By this time, Carl was utilizing nationally known auction companies to conduct his sales. An article on used farm equipment trends in the March 7, 1974, issue of *Implement & Tractor* magazine featured a Wenger's auction, conducted in Myerstown by the Midwest Auction Co., of Grand Meadows, Minnesota.

In addition to attracting local farmers—both Plain and more worldly—the 1974 auction drew dealers from about a dozen states, including as far away as Texas, Colorado, and South Dakota. The article noted that, while a year or two earlier, the flow of used equipment was from west to east, the current trend was from east to west. The top buyer for the day spent $104,000 on 19 tractors, which he trucked to his Texas dealership.

All told, 1,120 bidders purchased 165 tractors, 55 trucks and trailers, and 125 pieces of construction equipment, not to mention hundreds of used implements. There were so many pieces to be moved that selling time on some items was less than a minute. The most expensive piece, sold to an Indiana dealer, was a Case 2470 tractor that brought $22,700. Total bids for the day reached $1.48 million.

When his barn burned to the ground in April 1977, Carl used the insurance money to construct a warehouse.

The article noted the steady growth of Wenger's, which grossed just under $2 million in 1972, $3.25 million in 1973, and was shooting for $5 million in 1974.

Along the way, Carl added buildings to house his expanding business. When his barn burned on April 3, 1977, he used the insurance money to construct a warehouse. Lost in the fire were some equipment and parts, but family members were able to save 50 head of cattle and some horses from the flames.

A nearby Case dealer began dealing in Butler buildings, so Carl traded him some Case tractors for a pair of the steel buildings to accommodate his expanding business.

Going FFAing: A Family Tradition

As his sons entered their teen years, Carl's involvement in Future Farmers of America deepened. "My wife always made the statement that others do various things like golfing, fishing, or whatever," says Carl, "but we just went FFAing."

All four sons were active at the local, county, state, and national levels. Lloyd (1971), Larry (1975), Dave (1981), and Glenn (1983) each earned the national American Farmer Degree, and Lloyd, Dave, and Glenn also each were recognized as Eastern Regional Star Agri-Businessman. Despite three chances, Carl never was able to vicariously realize his dream by having a family member earn the American Star Farmer/Agri-Businessman award.

Caught up in the excitement of Lloyd's Regional Star Award in 1971, Carl prepared to go FFAing in a big way. He decided to buy a motor coach at an auction in Downingtown for family and friends to take to Kansas City, where Lloyd would receive his award at the October 12-15 National FFA Convention. "After I bought it," Carl recalls, "I suddenly realized I had never driven one before."

Going "FFAing" is a Wenger family tradition. Above are Carl's four sons in the late 1970s, sporting their FFA jackets: (from left) Davey, Larry, Lloyd, and Glenn. (Below) Lloyd and his new bride, Kitty, pose with Carl and Margaret in Kansas City, where Lloyd was recognized as Regional Star Agri-Businessman in 1971.

He soon found himself trapped, with a utility pole in front and a lot of impatient drivers behind him. Rescued by a driver of another coach, Carl managed to get his coach home. After painting it in FFA Blue and Gold, family and friends "FFAed" across the country in style. Immediately upon his return from Kansas City, 175 people attended a surprise party in Lloyd's honor at ELCO High School Auditorium, including county and state FFA officers.

Beginning when Glenn was state FFA vice-president, Carl and Margaret began hosting the FFA officers' meeting at their cabin on Blue Mountain each year, a pattern that has continued for nearly 30 years. Glenn continued on after his high school career, remaining active in the Pennsylvania FFA Foundation, which helps to organize reunions of past state officers.

Along with accolades and awards that they received, Carl's sons gained valuable experience and skills that would serve them well in their careers. Through FFA they learned to manage projects, keep meticulous records, communicate clearly, and work with others toward common goals.

Guiding all four boys through their FFA careers was Eastern Lebanon County (ELCO) High School agriculture teacher Gerald Strickler. The Wengers and Mr. Strickler shared mutual bonds of appreciation. When Glenn was competing for national office at the 1984 FFA convention in Kansas City, the Wengers surprised Mr. Strickler by flying his wife to the event.

At Mr. Strickler's final local FFA banquet in April 1994, the Wengers had another surprise in store. In gratitude for his years of service to school and community, Carl and Margaret gave the Stricklers a retirement gift of a trip to Florida and the Daytona 500.

Wenger's benefitted from the leadership skills that the boys developed in FFA, and FFA has benefitted through the years from generous support from Carl and the business from the local to the national level. Since his early days, Carl has had ongoing involvement with FFA, sponsoring the medals for county competitions, frequently attending auctions to make sure youth received a good return on their animals, and more. Carl is proud to have donated to the National FFA Foundation for more than 40 consecutive years.

Both the business and Carl and Margaret, personally, have received various recognitions from FFA through the years, including honorary American Farmer degrees presented to Carl and Margaret in 1971 and 1981, respectively.

The Wenger family would enjoy another round of success with FFA, when granddaughter Molly Jo Walmer served as the 2009-2010 President of the 8,000-member State FFA Association. She was awarded her American Degree in October 2011 at the 84th National FFA Convention in Indianapolis.

Cars for Kids

As his children reached driving age, Carl remembered how grateful he was for the car his father had provided for him, and he decided to carry on the tradition. "When the seven children became 16," says Lloyd, "we all pretty much got a car. We didn't have to pay for it. It was a company-owned car. And six of the seven of us wrecked them." (Only Nancy avoided this rite of passage.)

Just as his father had been patient with him when he made mistakes, Carl took his children's auto accidents in stride. "Dad would never say a word," says Lloyd. "He would never get angry." He would simply ask if the driver was okay and where to send the rollback truck to retrieve the wrecked car and driver. Some of the kids wrecked more than one, but the driver always walked away.

Lloyd experienced the same patience from his dad as he grew into the business. "Carl would try to correct you if he saw you doing something wrong," says Lloyd, "but he never

General-Lee Speaking

Generally speaking, Carl's kids' cars came and went without much fanfare. But one vehicle stood out from the others. In 1980, when the Dukes of Hazzard television show was popular, Lloyd partnered with Brian Boyer, of Boyer Signs, to paint a Dodge Charger identical to the General Lee that Bo, Luke, and Daisy used to elude Roscoe P. Coltrane and Boss Hogg on the back roads of Hazzard County, Kentucky. Wenger's General Lee was identical to the television version, right down to the engine, wheels, and interior. The only major difference was that the Wengers didn't weld their doors shut.

hollered at you or beat at you or got angry. He would try to straighten it out some other way."

Even when the kids weren't wrecking their cars, they learned to hold on to them loosely, because pretty much everything the company owned was for sale if the right deal came along. "I went through quite a few cars there for a little bit," Lloyd recalls. "You didn't get too attached to things. He would deal anything, anywhere, anytime. It didn't matter."

Youngest daughter Rose remembers how she lost her first car—a green Chrysler Cordoba that was handed down to her from one of her older brothers. One Friday after school she drove it to the office to work for a few hours, answering phones. Her dad commandeered it for the evening so some clients from New York could get around. The following morning Lloyd told Rose to clean out all her stuff. The car was sold. "It was my car, you know?" Rose recalls with a laugh. But it was gone.

Learning from Others

While Carl was a savvy businessman himself, and benefitted from the wisdom of his father, he also looked to other successful entrepreneurs as mentors. In the Myerstown area, he admired Carlos R. Leffler, who in 1941—at just 17 years of age—had borrowed $380 from his father to buy a truck to haul fertilizer, coal, and milk for Lebanon County farmers. He soon added fuel oil deliveries and eventually expanded his business into a conglomerate of coal- and petroleum-related enterprises, including heating oil and gasoline sales, heating and air conditioning, gas stations, convenience stores, and more. Carl would serve on the Board of Directors of the Lebanon Valley Brethren Home with Carlos and openly admired his business acumen. Ten years Carl's senior, Carlos would later be there for Carl at one of his greatest times of need.

Carl also counted Charlotte, North Carolina, auction company owner Chick Godley as a valuable mentor. Godley and his wife, Margaret, had fled the dust bowl depression of Colorado in 1935, eventually settling in Charlotte, where he and his sons grew a small livestock auction business into one of the largest independent auction companies in the Southeast. Their philosophy—"A lot of people dream of success and we wake up every day and work hard at achieving it"—resonated with Carl.

The multimillionaire took a shine to Carl. After a day at Godley's Auction, Chick would invite Carl to stay on, and the next day they would travel together in his wife's Lincoln to farm auctions. Godley gave Carl the keys to the Lincoln, along with much valuable advice. "He was always good to talk to," says Carl. "I know he said, 'Wenger, the first million was the hardest.' That was before I knew what a million dollars was."

Another mentor was Jim Vaughn, who owned the auction company in Stilesville, Indiana, that Carl frequented. Carl remembers passing Vaughn's company on his way to the 1953

FFA Convention in Kansas City, marveling at the impressive inventory. Little did he know that he would become one of Vaughn's biggest customers. Vaughn always treated Carl well and was gracious in working out payment details. When Vaughn died unexpectedly of a heart attack, says Carl, the funeral director had to get special racks to accommodate all of the flowers that people gave to honor the popular equipment dealer.

Carl also appreciated Tim Yoder from the Yoder & Frey Auction Company in Archbold. In between buying tractors, Carl spent many hours sitting in a truck, soaking in Tim's wisdom. "I would get in the truck with Tim and he would just tell me things," Carl remembers fondly. "He would keep me excited enough for the next two weeks. And then I was back again and would talk some more. He just took a liking to me, and they would cater to me and help me, just cheering me along."

Carl counts friendships with men like Leffler, Godley, Vaughn, and Yoder as some of his greatest accomplishments, and hopes some day younger folks will remember him as fondly as he remembers his mentors.

8

Troubling Times

The late 1960s and early 1970s were a period of rapid growth for Wenger's Farm Machinery. Growth required capital, which meant borrowing money. But a combination of factors—including overextending himself on credit, bad loans to customers, a sharp downturn in the economy accompanied by an unexpected spike in interest rates, and a Mack truck deal gone sour—resulted in multiple crises that threatened the future of the business and Carl's own mental and physical health. Before the ship would be righted, Carl would endure many sleepless nights, fall into a deep depression, and lose four valuable farms.

Credit Crunch

While Carl had learned much about business from his father, their attitudes toward credit were polar opposites. As a child of the Great Depression, John was averse to borrowing money. "I don't think John ever borrowed any money for anything," explains Lloyd. "Anything he bought he paid for right away. He was afraid to borrow money. And when dad came along, he was just the opposite. He would finance anything anywhere."

When things got especially tight, Carl would sometimes stoop to some creative financing of his own. "In his early years he had cash flow problems," understates Larry. The "early years" extended into the 1970s and '80s.

To cover cash shortages, Carl sometimes floated checks, says Lloyd. He wrote checks on accounts with insufficient funds, but understood how the banks worked well enough that he could cover one account with a check from another and keep his house of cards from collapsing.

"He had it figured out when the bank would cash the checks," explains Lloyd, "and he would float money between banks and customers. He didn't have it, but he kept writing checks different ways and making it work."

At other times, the business was behind on its payments to suppliers. Larry remembers during the late 1970s that his dad would have the secretary write out checks to pay bills and place them in a drawer. Monitoring his bank accounts, he would let the secretary know each day which bills she could pay. If a supplier would pressure Carl for an overdue payment, that check would get bumped ahead of some others. Some weeks Carl scrambled to meet payroll, as well.

While he managed to keep things afloat most of the time, he wasn't always successful. Dave remembers the embarrassment of going to pick up parts at a local supplier and being refused service because Wenger's was behind on its payments. And Carl also was having trouble with banks.

Carl began banking with Schaefferstown First National Bank (which later merged with Lebanon Valley National Bank), where his father had served on the board for many years. But by the early 1960s his customer notes and operational needs exceeded the small local bank's lending limits. The bottom line was that one day Carl got a call from the bank, notifying him that he was over his credit limit and his hometown bank was unable to extend further credit, effective immediately. Carl was in a bind.

"I had never physically set foot in another bank," he explains, "but I had to go shopping. I had checks written and notes on my desk with no money to operate." Widening his circle of credit, he established relationships with Lebanon County Trust and Berks County Trust to obtain money for his cash-starved business. Both institutions handled his third party debt for a time, allowing Carl to extend credit to his customers. The downside was that Carl was still liable for any bad debt that his customers created for him. He had operating capital to keep going, but he also had assumed greater risk.

"I would just get these notes and this paper and go to bank by the bushel baskets," Carl recalls. "They didn't check credits and I didn't check credits and this thing got out of hand."

Because he had signed recourse papers, the bank held him responsible for farmers who failed to pay off their equipment loans.

Carl needed more money to operate his business, and decided to mortgage his property to get it. On his 35th birthday, in May 1967, Berks County Trust agreed to a $500,000 mortgage. He remembers feeling satisfied when accountant friend John Good told him, "There are very few 35-year-olds who can go out and borrow a half million dollars."

But while Carl thought he was getting the half million for operations, when the papers were signed, half of the mortgage went to cover the bad paper, representing customers' unpaid bills, leaving Carl with half of the operating funds he thought he was getting, and a couple hundred thousand dollars of notes that were his responsibility to collect. In November 1967, some of that "bad paper" would go to John and Bertha as part of the transfer of the business from John to Carl, Margaret, and the family. For a time, John and Bertha became the collection agency for the bad debt.

While it wasn't entirely what he was seeking, the infusion of cash from the mortgage stabilized things for a time, and allowed the business to grow. Carl continued to cast a wider net, seeking financing to expand, but the nature of his business hindered him. "Carlos Leffler used to say, 'Get a banker that will work with you,'" says Carl. "Well, I couldn't, because no one wanted to work with used equipment. One time I had one of our local bankers drive by our lot and he said that they should just load up all of that junk and take it to the scrap yard. The bankers always wanted to finance the shiny new stuff, not the used stuff. If I wouldn't have been sitting on the real estate, I wouldn't have had any equity. They couldn't see equity in the equipment."

Debt and Depression

After Carl had dealt with some other local banks, in the early 1970s a Philadelphia bank that was seeking to widen its service area agreed to loan money to Wenger's Farm Machinery. "They got a good [Pennsylvania] Dutch guy from Lancaster County, and they were going to expand in Lancaster and Berks Counties," Carl explains. "They wanted my business and I gave it to them."

They extended him an $850,000 line of credit, and were on the verge of increasing the line by another half million dollars, when things suddenly changed. Some of the bank's investments elsewhere went sour, and they needed cash. They decided to collect from customers who were located furthest from Philadelphia first, which put Carl in their crosshairs.

While he had yet to receive the $500,000 credit line

Serious financial stress during the 1970s threatened Carl's business and his mental health.

increase, Carl was anticipating the increase would be granted the following week, so he had stretched his resources. But instead of the increase he was expecting, the bank suddenly called in the entire $850,000 loan, putting him on a $10,000/week repayment schedule. Carl signed over a life insurance policy as additional collateral. They switched him to a less accommodating loan officer and began to play hardball.

Carl held an auction to raise some of the money in the early 1970s, but an uneasy feeling permeated the event, as clipboard-toting bank representatives hovered over the proceedings. The auction was less than successful. Carl worked at repaying the debt for close to a year, making obligatory 75-mile trips to meet with bank representatives in Philadelphia every few weeks. The meetings made Carl so angry that he had someone ride along because he didn't trust himself to ride alone. "Once I came out of a meeting so disturbed that the secretary was afraid to hand me my coat," Carl laments. "I can still see her reaching it out to me as far as her arms could reach."

A favorite tactic of the bank, says Carl, was to call on a Friday afternoon, threatening that they would be out the following Monday to take the keys to the property, which made for many sleepless weekends. The bank actually took action to foreclose on the business, but their effort was thwarted by Lebanon County Judge John Walter, who ruled that there was sufficient collateral. The bank was required to allow Carl to continue making payments.

Carl offered to hold another auction in fall 1975, but the bank insisted that they receive all revenue, even from the sale of consigned items, which Carl couldn't do because he didn't own those pieces.

After many months of extreme stress, things came to a head when the bank came after Lloyd. Carl's 24-year-old son had signed on the loan for 10 percent of the indebtedness. Carl remembers going to a local stock club he was part of on a

Wednesday evening. He was so disturbed that he couldn't think straight and left the meeting early. "I laid awake all night, trying to figure out how to get away from the bank."

The following morning he reviewed his life insurance policy. (He had signed his life insurance over to the bank as part of his indebtedness, so they had a stake.) Then he sat down and wrote a desperate letter to the bank, offering them a clear choice: They could give him time to hold an auction on his terms to raise money to repay the loan, or they could collect the money from his life insurance policy.

Clearly not thinking straight, Carl had decided to offer his life to preserve the business. "I spent my whole life building this business for the kids," Carl explained in a 2009 interview, "and I wasn't going to let the bank have it. If I had to give up my life to let the business for the kids, it was going to be that way. That may not be good thinking, but that is the way it was. It's the truth."

In a 2011 interview, Carl softened his account of the desperate situation. He said he never was suicidal, but he wrote the letter to the bank to offer them a clear choice. They could either give him time to pay his debts or pay a much larger death claim. "I figured the insurance company would rather loan me the money than pay the death claim," he said.

The recipients of the letter had no way of knowing whether Carl was bluffing. When the letter arrived the phone started ringing. Carl's insurance agent and friend, Al Hicks, promptly took him to Hershey Medical Center for a psychiatric evaluation. They returned home to find a concerned Margaret, Carlos Leffler, and John Good waiting for them. Given Carl's unsettling ultimatum, the bank chose the auction, which was held in fall 1975. It came up $40,000 short of repaying the remainder of the $850,000 loan.

Still distraught, Carl got into his office late on December 23, 1975. There on his desk he found three checks, one for

$20,000 from Carlos Leffler and two for $10,000 each from attorney Walter Whitmoyer and Al Hicks. Beside the checks was a brief note urging Carl to have a good Christmas. His friends thought that he had worked hard enough to repay his debts. He could pay them back as he was able. Carl settled the bank loan the same day, lifting a tremendous burden from his shoulders. It was Carl and Margaret's 25th wedding anniversary. A short time later, Carl, Margaret, and Rose went away for a few days. Carl recalls, "Rosie asked me why I went away when all I did was sleep." What she didn't understand at the time was that Carl hadn't had a good night's sleep for nearly a year.

The following year, on Thanksgiving Day, Carl confessed to his family how he had gotten out from under the bank. "The tears really flowed that holiday with all of our children present at the home of my parents," Carl remembers. Carl cancelled his life insurance policy and bought new policies that wouldn't cover suicide for an initial two-year period so that he wouldn't be tempted to do something rash again.

Though he was freed from bondage to the Philadelphia bank, Wenger's Farm Machinery wasn't out of the woods. Carl and the business remained unstable, as the economy went into recession and Carl into deeper depression. For four years, the embittered businessman contemplated taking legal recourse against the bank, which he figured had treated him unfairly, costing the business as much as a million dollars. He eventually decided against legal action.

Meanwhile, interest rates in the late 1970s spiked to 20 percent or higher, bringing the economy to a grinding halt. "He had a lot of borrowed money, and we had a lot of inventory," Lloyd recalls. "That was very hard on him."

In fall 1979 Carl couldn't take it anymore and stepped away from the day-to-day operation of the business. He handed over the presidency of the company to Lloyd, who was still shy of his 30th birthday. While Lloyd concentrated on selling tractors and equipment to help rescue the company from its dire straits, Carl wasn't fit to deal with customers. For several months, he spent his days doing nothing but physical labor out behind the buildings, while Lloyd held things together inside.

Four Fewer Farms

When he returned to his desk the following spring, his financial woes continued. Over time Carl had accumulated several farms and refinanced four of them with a single mortgage, making for a "pretty stiff" mortgage payment. As the farm economy sagged, the farms weren't breaking even, and had to be subsidized by the farm equipment business, which was generating modest profits. Carl invested in a new dairy barn on a Rehrersburg-area farm, only to see it burn to the ground in August 1980. The loss was estimated at $100,000. He built a second barn, resulting in further indebtedness. Under normal circumstances, he would have been able to weather the storm, by using profits from the farm machinery to continue making farm payments, all the while with the farms appreciating in value 15 percent annually.

But these were not normal circumstances. "The interest rates got high and the farm equipment business didn't get 'Spring Fever,'" Carl explains. "There is only one year that ever happened. I was loaded with big tractors, and I couldn't get anyone to walk from my office down to the field to even look at them, much less buy them."

So he fell behind in his payments on the farms' mortgage.

Complicating things further was a partnership with another businessman Carl entered into in 1979 to purchase some off-road Mack dump trucks. Mack was phasing them out and was willing to sell the huge vehicles at a good price. Carl and his partner agreed to buy them on the half and share profits. But the economy and the deal went sour, leaving Carl with $400,000 sunk into trucks that he couldn't sell because businesses had frozen capital expenditures due to the sagging economy.

"If we had had those trucks 90 days earlier," Carl laments, "we could have sold them at a profit. And 90 days after we bought them, we never would have looked at them. But right then was the exact wrong time."

At several points in the late 1970s and early 1980s, Wenger's held special auctions to raise cash to keep the banks at bay. One crisis struck in February 1979, when Carl and Margaret were away on a trip to the People's Republic of China. "The bank called a pretty big note," says Lloyd. So Lloyd scheduled an auction to raise the needed cash.

The day before the auction a major snowstorm buried everything. "We had a whole big field of machinery lined up," explains Lloyd. "We couldn't sell it because we couldn't see it. We couldn't get to it. All of our equipment, our cultipackers and disks and stuff, were covered." What's more, the drifted roads were impassable so that local buyers couldn't get to the sale. Fortunately, most of the out-of-state buyers had come in before the storm and were staying nearby in hotels.

Lloyd called the bank and explained he couldn't get all the money because of the weather. They understood, but urged Lloyd to do what he could. Then he contacted the buyers in area hotels and let them know they would have an auction, but it would start late and include tractors only, no other machinery. Then they began digging out tractors and sold as many as they could extract from the snowdrifts. The bank was satisfied with their efforts.

Despite their best efforts, after two years, Carl was a full year behind on farm payments, and the lender had had enough. In 1983, he surrendered all four farms, totaling about 400 acres, and agreed to repay $200,000 to get out from the obligation. Carl paid dearly for over-extending himself.

Dumb Name, Smart Profit

Carl always was on the lookout for a good deal, even when he was on vacation. He and Margaret traveled to Asia for three weeks in fall 1972 as Good Will Ambassadors with an agriculture-oriented People to People tour group. The trip included stops in Japan, the Philippines, Thailand, Hong Kong, and Taiwan. While the group toured Taiwan, the ubiquitous 10-speed bicycles caught Carl's eye. He thought he could sell some reasonably priced bikes back in the states.

After a busy day of sightseeing, Carl hailed a cab on his own in the evening and visited bicycle factories. Unable to speak with management during his evening visits and hindered by the language barrier, Carl simply handed out a few business cards and communicated as best he could that he would be interested in buying some bikes.

About six weeks later two young Taiwanese men, who were studying in the States, showed up in Myerstown one Saturday afternoon. Carl agreed to buy a thousand bikes, sending some of the payment to Taiwan and giving some to the students. That way the students had spending money in the U.S. and their parents, who owned the factory, didn't have to pay taxes on the full transaction.

Some time later three containers of Luck Star 10-speed bikes arrived at Baltimore Harbor. "They were not Lucky Star," clarifies Lloyd. "They were Luck Star. It was a dumb name."

But they were good, cheap bikes, and new 10-speeds were becoming popular. Carl thinks they may have paid about $35 a piece, and he could sell them for double that and still easily under-price area dealers. Carl put the boys to work, setting up bikes, and advertised in *Lancaster Farming*.

Soon vanloads of Plain Mennonites from Lancaster County began showing up. Six or eight Mennonites would pile out of the van, each purchase a bike, and ride them 20 or more miles home. "These things sold easy," Lloyd recalls. "It was fun for a while."

Carl believes they sold the first two thirds the first year and the rest the following year. "People were fighting over them."

Carl and Margaret participated in a second trip to Asia in February 1979, this time as part of the Pennsylvania Agricultural Leaders Goodwill Delegation to the People's Republic of China. In August 1979, Carl and Margaret then hosted a delegation of 12 agricultural leaders from a communal farm in China, who were visiting the U.S. through the U.S.-China People's Friendship Association to learn more about dairy machinery and mechanization. Carl and Margaret served up a clambake for their guests and gave them a tour of their farm and business.

"I had a million dollars less debt on Thursday evening than I had Thursday morning," Carl recalls.

He also had considerably fewer assets. He estimates those same farms today might be worth $4 million. Most painful was the loss of a farm near Stouchburg that had belonged to Carl's father. To this day, Carl avoids driving past those farms and the painful memories they represent.

While Carl still feels the sting of those losses, he is able to reflect philosophically. He observes, "When you have success, it often comes in small bites, but when you have mistakes, they come in big chunks. That is just the way it is."

The Villsmeier Auction

While the loss of the farms reduced Carl's debt, the equipment business still had another bank loan with high interest rates hanging over its head. Attempts to renegotiate more favorable terms for the loan had been unsuccessful and the cloud of debt loomed ominously over the business.

Carl's son, Glenn, who by the mid-1980s was assuming a larger role and later would become President, recalls sitting down with his father and attorney Walter Whitmoyer early in 1984 to discuss how to resolve the debt crisis once and for all.

They resolved to hold a special public auction the first weekend of April. The Villsmeier Auction Company from Montgomeryville, Pennsylvania, conducted the memorable two-day sale, selling "every piece regardless of what it brought," says Lloyd.

"We sold 90 percent of our inventory," echoes Glenn, "and we wrote the bank a check, paid them to zero, and we were out of debt."

Improving Outlook

Reflecting on the challenges the business and the family faced in the late 1970s and early 1980s, Lloyd observes, "We got through every time. But it was a family. . . . Everyone worked together. No one threw their hands up and said, 'Hey we don't want to do it anymore.' We all just worked together."

"I would not have wanted to come into the business at any other time," adds Glenn, "because I learned a lot through that experience. I always felt fortunate that I came into the business in a down time."

With debt problems resolved, Wenger's Farm Machinery had a clean slate and could begin to rebuild the business. Its best years were yet to come, with a major expansion and relocation still on the horizon.

As the business climate improved, so did Carl's outlook on life. Over time he would regain his mental health and reinvest himself in his business. Beyond that, he would begin to invest more of his energy in philanthropic efforts and would find returns on those investments perhaps even more satisfying than his more familiar business profits.

9

Wenger's, Inc.: A Business on the Rise

Having come through the struggles of the late 1970s and early 1980s, Carl and the business regained their footing during the 1980s. Though Carl had been chastened by his financial losses and personal struggles, the business was profitable and poised for growth. Even before the big Villsmeier auction in spring 1984, Wenger's was doing considerable business.

A 1983 aerial photo shows an expanding business, including several new buildings that were added since the previous aerial photo had been taken in the early 1970s.

A January 1981 news story reported that Wenger's was shipping equipment to 48 states and Canada and acquiring used equipment from farmers and auctions in 30 states. Lloyd reported that Wenger's held six auctions per year, and more than half of the firm's business was with out-of-state dealers.

A January 1982 *Reading Eagle* newspaper article reported that Wenger's employed 15 people—five working full-time tearing down tractors—carried a $2 million inventory, and had become "one of the largest used parts dealers east of the Mississippi."

In addition to tractors and equipment, tractor parts, and construction equipment, in the early 1980s Wenger's fueled growth by adding a construction parts salvage operation. As they had done with tractors for many years, they now began disassembling earth moving equipment and marketing used parts.

Growing out of Carl's personal struggles, in 1980 the business announced a new name and leadership structure with more prominent roles for the children. The business now would be known as Wenger's, Inc. Lloyd continued as President and Sales Manager, Larry was named Vice-President and Treasurer, 20-year-old Davey assumed the role of Vice President in Charge of Purchasing, and Nancy served as Secretary. Carl exerted influence from his position as Chairman of the Board.

In his new role, Davey traveled extensively to equipment auctions throughout the eastern United States. A program for a local FFA banquet in March 1982 noted that Davey had purchased more than 200 tractors and 300 pieces of equipment for the business during the previous two years and was spending up to 80 percent of his time on the road attending machinery auctions.

Davey wasn't the only family member attending auctions, however. In 1985, Carl and Margaret had built a home in Deltona, Florida, and began to spend each February there. In 1990 they purchased a beautiful brick home in DeLand—with

Carl and Margaret bought a beautiful brick home in DeLand, Florida, in 1990 that served as a home base for attending auctions and auto races.

plenty of space to host family and friends—and began to spend a larger portion of the winter in the south. Of course, Carl didn't go to Florida to fish or play golf. From their southern home base, Carl scoured a number of equipment auctions in Florida and neighboring states for equipment.

Off to the Races

In addition to providing Carl easy access to southern auctions, the Florida home had the added advantage of being a short distance from the Daytona Speedway, where Carl became a fixture at the Daytona 500 each February. Carl and Margaret have hosted many family members and friends through the years, who have had the opportunity to participate in Carl's race day ritual and love of NASCAR.

It actually begins well in advance of race day, when Carl handles arrangements and purchases tickets for the Wenger contingent. On race Sunday, Carl always drives, parks in the grass at a spot reserved for him at the Friendly's restaurant across the street from the race track, and enjoys a hearty breakfast and a hug from his favorite waitress.

Florida friend Dave Miller has experienced the ritual. "While living only 20 miles from the Daytona track," writes Dave, "I always said I wouldn't go to the races unless I had a good seat and someone else drove. Well, Carl came through on both counts."

After breakfast, Carl and contingent head across the street to the track, where he is instantly recognizable to longtime employees. Linda Dixon met Carl through handling his ticket purchases. Carl quickly transformed the relationship into a friendship, and greeting Linda became part of the annual race-day ritual.

"The picture I see when I think of Carl Wenger," writes Linda, "is a man walking up to the counter in the Ticket Office at Daytona Speedway with a big hat and a bigger smile on his face, always carrying a large box of Pennsylvania pretzels."

(Linda admits that for many years she thought Carl owned a pretzel company, but pretzels are one commodity that Carl never dealt in. He has, however, used Lebanon County's Shuey's Pretzels as tools to win friends and influence people, keeping a stock of the salty delicacy on hand for everyday use and special occasions.)

Following a day enjoying the roar of the engines and the thrill of the race, it is back to Friendly's for another meal and, if he's lucky, another hug from the waitress that has been serving Carl and friends for many years. Longtime friend and race companion Bud Mitstifer says that some race days they managed to eat all three meals at Friendly's, which likely more than paid for their parking privileges.

Carl's love of racing wasn't limited to Daytona. When youngest son, Davey, developed an interest in fast cars, Carl was eager to help foot the bills and became a huge fan. The Wengers got into racing in 1974, when Lloyd purchased a Volkswagen mini-stock car and started racing on local tracks. Davey served on Lloyd's pit crew.

"I bought a race car and started going racing," Lloyd recalls. "And it was fun. We ran for a couple years, but then our kids came along. Then one weekend I blew two engines in one weekend. I said, 'That's it, I quit.' Davey said, 'Can I have the car?' I said, 'Sure take it.' And he started going and he did a lot better at it than I did."

Davey started racing when he was just 15, so he had to get a ride to the races, since he couldn't drive legally on the roads.

"I could race once I was there," he explains, "but I couldn't get there. Even when I turned 16 I could drive (to the track), but I had a 'Cinderella license.' I couldn't drive home after midnight." Friend Susie Deck proved a reliable source of transportation to and from the races for a time.

With Davey behind the wheel, beginning in the mid-1970s, Carl took interest and sponsored Wenger Brothers Racing, Inc., becoming a huge backer and fan. Davey and his support team used Wenger's shop and tools to maintain their cars and build a successful racing team.

For the next 20 years racing played a prominent role in Wenger family summer weekends. Davey drove a circuit that included clay tracks at Big Diamond Raceway, near Pottsville, on Friday night; Grandview Speedway, Bechtelsville, on Saturday; and Penn National, Grantville, on Sunday. In 1986, alone, Wenger Brothers Racing participated in 75 races at Pennsylvania tracks. Davey won the 1987 Tri-Track Championship in small block modified, and was points champion at Grandview Speedway in 1994. Along the way he graduated from the VW mini-stock to a small block car with a Chevy engine.

"Dad would go to all the races," remembers Rose, "and the rest of us would fit in whenever we felt like going." Penn National—which no longer hosts car races—was the biggest attraction and usually drew the largest crowds.

Davey, flanked by his parents, at Penn National in 1987.

Davey, his wife-to-be Gwen Miller, Carl, and Margaret in the winner's circle at the annual Freedom 76 run at Grandview Speedway, 1987.

Grandson Justin Wenger remembers spending weekend summer afternoons at his grandparents' swimming pool. Carl would leave for the races late afternoon. "The van was always open," says Justin. "If you were there at the right time when he was ready to go, there was always a ride to the races."

In addition to the local races, Davey also raced in New York, New Jersey, Delaware, and even Florida. Bashore Trucking eventually became a partner in sponsoring the team, and then took over the operation in the late 1990s. Carl's relationship to racing and the Bashores continued when the Bashores became part owners of Big Diamond Raceway and gave Carl some free tickets to come to the races. The first time he went, Carl enjoyed the experience, but there were some hurdles to overcome.

Parlaying a Pool

Carl and Margaret ended up with an in ground pool in their yard when, following in his father's footsteps, Lloyd parlayed a skid loader into a pool. Carl and Margaret weren't much interested in a pool, but the kids were. When a short-on-cash representative from a Palmyra-area pool dealer inquired about buying a skid loader, Lloyd worked a deal for a pool next to his parents' farmhouse. The contractor came in the fall to dig the hole for the pool in the lower part of the yard and struck water—which would have been good for a pond, but wasn't so good for a pool. They let it sit and installed the pool on higher ground the following spring. Not one to waste an opportunity, Rose remembers ice skating with neighborhood kids on the temporary pond in the yard that winter. Skating was just for one season, but the pool would provide many years of enjoyment for Carl and Margaret's children and grandchildren.

"I came home and told them, 'Thank you, I liked all of it,'
Carl recalls. 'I'll come back racing again. But I need to have my
tickets at Myerstown—I don't want to stand in line. I need to
have a place to park—my walking on that rough stuff just isn't
so good.' So the next time I got up there, there's a cardboard
sign, 'Parking for Carl Wenger Only.' I parked there and a couple weeks later there was a nice painted sign. It's been there for
a number of years."

With VIP parking in place, Davey took care of the tickets by
selling the Speedway some equipment and getting a stack of tickets thrown in as payment. Two cheap plastic chairs with "Wenger"
scrawled on them were set out each week, completing the package
and setting the stage for many Friday nights at the races.

Dentist Richard Bohn has been one of Carl's regular racing
companions at Big Diamond and has many fond memories of
"pigging out" on racetrack food and enjoying the night out with
Carl and friends. "He has a heart of gold," says Doc Bohn. "I
don't think I've paid for any tickets since I've gone up there."
Doc's contribution to the trips, in addition to providing good
company, was to pick up the French fries at the food stand and
then take the wheel for the late night drive home. But one time
Carl even had to help him with that.

"I do have a little bit of a lead foot," Doc confesses. When
he got pulled over for speeding by a local policeman around
Pine Grove, it was Carl who took care of it. "I just figured if
anybody could talk us out of it, Carl could," Doc says with a
laugh. "And he did!"

Reaching Out

As his business became more profitable, Carl became more
involved in community service and philanthropy. Spurred in
part by the example of other successful businessmen and the

Easy Come, Easy Go

Wenger Brothers Racing was far from a money-making operation. And it didn't help when Carl gave away the winnings. It was September 1979. Davey had just won first place in the Mid-Atlantic VW Sprint Championship Race at Georgetown, Delaware. After loading up his car and equipment, Davey hurried toward the payoff window to collect his hard-earned $250 purse. But Carl intercepted him on the way, informed Davey that he had already obtained the prize money . . . and had given it away!

"I was so proud of myself," Davey recalls. "You know, I was 19 years old and I won this race. And Dad's giving my prize money away before I even get to see it."

Davey had intended to put the money back into the car, but the race was being run in memory of a man who had died in an accident. When a collection was taken up for the man's family, Carl contributed the Wenger winnings.

Davey didn't get his purse, but he did get a life lesson and to this day has a hand-written thank you letter from the widow who received the gift.

"But that was his thing," Davey concludes. "Somebody else needed it more than we did. And Dad knew that. I didn't feel that way at the time it was happening, but as you get a little older you understand."

kindness that had been shown to him in hard times, Carl began to give more. He always had been a generous supporter of FFA, but he began to expand his giving to a wider variety of church and community organizations.

In 1979, Carl, Margaret, and Carl's mother, Bertha, gave a memorial gift to the Midway Church of the Brethren in honor

Carl's mother, Bertha Wenger, taught Sunday school for many years at Midway Church of the Brethren.

of Carl's father to provide padding for the church pews. The church had been a spiritual comfort to the Wengers over John's passing, and the Wengers' donation would provide physical comfort for church members for decades to come. Carl later would serve as the Treasurer of the Midway Church.

In 1980, Carl accepted an invitation to serve on the board of the Church of the Brethren's fledgling Lebanon Valley Brethren Home, which had opened its doors in February 1979. Prominent Brethren businessmen Bob DiMatteo, of ASK Foods, and Carlos Leffler helped Administrator Paul Boll persuade Carl to serve, beginning a decades-long relationship between the Wengers and the home. According to Paul, Carl was instrumental in establishing the home's Good Samaritan Fund and two major events to support the fund—a $100-a-plate benefit dinner and a chicken barbeque and auction. Carl credits Carlos Leffler as the driving force behind the dinner, but Carl played an especially prominent role in the auction. Son Lloyd, his wife, Kitty, and other Wenger family members have followed in his footsteps.

The Brethren Disaster Relief Auction (BDRA), held annually at the Lebanon Expo Center, is another event that has benefitted greatly from Carl's support. Begun in 1977, the auction would develop into a fundraising juggernaut and the largest Church of the Brethren gathering anywhere in the U.S. A quilt auction, livestock auction, and lots of good food were early staples of the event.

With Carl's interests in agriculture, auctions, and eating, the BDRA was a natural place for him to get involved. Friends Dennis and Marti Shaak describe Carl as "a dynamic presence" at the auction and a "cheerleader for the auction mission."

As was the case with the Lebanon Valley Brethren Home, Carl again was inspired to greater involvement in the auction by his mentor Leffler. At the 1982 livestock sale at the auction, Leffler, Carl, and Victor Ziegler happened to be sitting together. The oilman Leffler purchased a calf for $550 and instructed the auctioneer to sell it again. Not to be outdone, Carl then purchased the same calf for $600 and donated it back. It sold a third time to Victor for $550, before being purchased for $450 by a dairy farmer.

Leffler explained to a reporter afterwards, "It wasn't planned. We were all sitting together and it just started. I said, 'Carl, it's your turn to bid now.' Then we told Victor it was his turn."

Even when Carl was struggling financially during the late 1970s, he chose to support the resettling of a Vietnamese family through the Midway Church of the Brethren. Touched by the plight of refugees who were coming to Fort Indiantown Gap, Carl attended a congregational business meeting at the Midway church to see what the church would decide to do. After the church agreed to sponsor one family, Carl offered to pay all expenses for a second family, providing the church took care of the details. "I had no money," Carl recalls, "but I figured, if I'm going to go down the tubes, one more family isn't going to make that much difference." In the end, Carl and the church split expenses for one family.

It wasn't the first, or last, time that Carl would be moved by a person in need and respond. Another episode took place in December 1985 at an auction at the Jones Farm Equipment Company in Dothan, Alabama. On the block that day were a number of pieces of farm equipment that had been repossessed by the Coffee County Bank from a farmer who had not met his obligations to the bank.

When bidding began on a Farmall H tractor, the owner's wife and son, obviously distraught, cried out against the sale of their family tractor. Initially, Carl began bidding on the tractor, but then dropped out. As soon as it sold to another bidder, Carl was conscience-stricken. He felt that he should have acted to save the tractor for the family. A friend attending the auction had the same idea, and eventually a third party joined in. They negotiated with the buyer to purchase the tractor at a profit to him. "We put our money together," says Carl, "went in the office and got a paid ticket, and came out, gave it to the young fellow and told him, 'Now, take your tractor back home.'"

A short time later, Carl received a letter from the bank President, praising Carl for his "noble act" and offering to contribute toward the purchase price of the tractor. While defending the bank's position, the President also expressed regret for "the trauma which the young man experienced during the sale." Carl chose not to accept the bank's help. "(The banker) was there and said he had a job he had to do," says Carl. "And that's alright. . . . But I had a job we had to do too, and that was take care of this woman and boy."

Community Minded

Closer to home, Carl and the family business increasingly were known as dependable community servants. Consistent with his support of disaster relief in the U.S. and abroad through the annual Brethren auction, Carl saw to it that people who experienced disasters close to home also were cared for. Friend Ken Wagner observes, "Whenever a fire occured in Eastern Lebanon County area, the following morning Carl would send employees and equipment to help clean up at no cost to the victims."

Ken experienced Carl's kindness firsthand in November 1983, when his home burned just before Thanksgiving. The next day the Wengers offered a place to live and a storage garage. The Wagners used both for several months while their new home was being built.

Carl also became a generous supporter of local fire companies. When the Myerstown Goodwill Fire Company purchased a new pumper truck in March 1978 for $62,000, Carl agreed to purchase the 1947 Mack pumper that they were replacing for $2,500. He then donated the old pumper to Myerstown's Keystone Fire Company for continued use.

Carl also built strong relationships with Myerstown Borough and Jackson Township municipal leaders and worked cooperatively to improve the community. "The relationship between the business and the borough and the township is just excellent," says Carl. "They will do anything for us and we will help them all we can."

Carl cites the reworking of an unsafe intersection at King Street and Route 501 on the southern edge of Myerstown as an example. Because of poor visibility due to a railroad overpass, the intersection was the site of frequent accidents. During the 1980s, Carl donated land to create a safer intersection. "That could be one of the best things we did," Carl says with satisfaction. In return, Jackson Township officials worked with Carl to bring the public water supply beyond the railroad underpass at Myerstown's southern edge to service property owned by the Wengers.

Similarly, when two tractor trailers rolled over on a dangerous curve south of Myerstown on Route 501, Carl again sprang into action, pressuring state officials to install warning signs. The signs were soon erected, sparing truckers future accidents.

Carl, and his sons after him, also frequently loaned equipment to both borough and township for road maintenance and construction projects. Dean Moyer, Chairman of the Jackson

Township Board of Supervisors, recalls, "If we needed a particular piece of equipment for a special project, Wenger's never let us down, providing what we needed at no cost to the Township."

Of course, occasionally loaner pieces came with strings attached. Jackson Township Road Foreman Brian Hoffman, writes, "One of Carl's goals was to get areas of weeds that needed to be cut. He would say, 'I will supply a tractor and you do the operating,' and I complied."

Carl continued to be a major presence at FFA and 4-H livestock auctions. A January 1980 *Lancaster Farming* article reported that Wenger's, Inc., purchased a full third of the steers sold at the Lebanon County Livestock 4-H Club roundup and sale, following Carl's longstanding practice of bidding on some of the lesser animals to make sure all participants received a good return on their investment.

All Fired Up

Carl wasn't interested only in helping fire companies put fires out. He also liked to light fires.

"I'm a great guy to clean up," he explains. "And an easy way to clean something up is to put a match to it. It kind of goes away." So Carl became known for lighting fires—big fires—to dispose of clutter and debris on his properties. Carl was reprimanded more than once by local authorities for his pyromaniac tendencies.

"They were there to reprimand me one day," he recalls, for starting unsafe fires. "A guy was in there reading me the riot act." Meanwhile, out back, unbeknownst to the official, Carl had a couple fires burning in the salvage yard.

Carl remembers another time when friends Clyde Deck and Roger Gerhart were flying in from Carlisle area in

Deck's plane. A huge plume of smoke caught their attention many miles away. Sure that it was a significant building fire, they followed the smoke, only to discover it was one of Carl's trash piles.

But that was a campfire, compared to Carl's biggest burn, which melted electric wires, incinerated railroad ties on an active track, and closed down a nearby factory.

Over time, a big hole in one of Carl's fields along King Street in Myerstown had grown into a dump, filled with old tractor tires, construction debris, and miscellaneous junk. One day Carl was working in that field on his tractor, and on impulse decided to take care of the unsightly heap.

"I got down to the end of the field," he recalls, "and I lit that son of a gun." Stirred by a breeze and fueled by hot-burning tires, the pile began to burn out of control. The heat was so intense that it melted the coating off of nearby utility wires, and set the ends of railroad ties on an active track to smoldering. Black, acrid smoke wafted toward the nearby Bayer aspirin plant, coating employees' cars with soot. When the air conditioning system began to draw in the fouled air, Bayer had to close the plant and send employees home. Cars stopped along the road to view the spectacle.

Knowing he was in trouble this time, Carl called the fire company and asked them to get a fire truck out there on the double—without turning on the siren. With the help of the fire company and a crawler to push the hole shut, the fire eventually was brought under control.

The only censure sheepish Carl received for the incident was the wrath of a responding fireman who, without knowing it was Carl, declared that whoever started the fire ought to be penned up.

Carl—and his children after him—has maintained good relationships with local munici-palities, often loaning equipment free of charge. Pictured here is a lot of equipment and the construction facility that was built in 1996.

Other Endeavors

In addition to his core business and community endeavors, Carl had begun to branch out into other ventures. Already in 1972, the family had formed a real estate holding corporation J K & B, Inc. Named after Carl's parents John K. and Bertha, the company developed a 139-acre farm in Huntingdon County, Pennsylvania, during the 1970s. In 1980 J K & B announced plans to develop a 97-acre Industrial Park on Wenger land at the south end of Myerstown.

Earlier Carl had partnered with attorney Walter Whitmoyer and real estate agent Joel Zinn to form ELCO Development, another real estate company. The company constructed and managed 24 apartments in Palmyra, along with other investment properties. "Back then we scratched money together," says Carl. "None of us had very much, but we just kept working at it, and we have a reasonable income off of it every year." Carl and his partners dissolved the 40-year-old partnership in December 2011, but continue to own a few properties jointly.

In 1977, Wenger's launched Wenger Leasing Company to handle specialized long-term financing for used farm equipment—an arena that traditional lending institutions sometimes were reticent to enter. The company was renamed Champion Leasing in 1995 and continues as an affiliate in the Wenger family of companies.

A Fresh Start

Following the Villsmeier auction in spring 1984, Wenger's was relieved of its debt issues, but it also had been relieved of most of its inventory. It was Carl's mentor and friend Carlos Leffler who exerted his influence to help get them up and running again. Not long after Wenger's had paid off their bank loan, Leffler, who sat on the bank board, and fellow board member Dick Bashore sought to win back the Wengers' business.

Glenn recalls that he and his dad met with the board members over lunch at the Dixie in Lebanon. Glenn picks up the story: "They said 'What must we do to get your business back?' I remember dad's comment: 'Well, we have a business. We have no inventory. We have no money.'

"And Carlos said, 'Well, how much do you need to get going?' And we said we ought to have a couple hundred thousand dollars so we could go buy some stuff and sell some stuff. And he said, 'Stop down at my office this afternoon and pick up a check for $200,000.' And that's what we did. So that got us back in business."

A short time later the bank expanded that initial loan to a larger line of credit and Wenger's was on the move again. Young Glenn took two valuable lessons from the experiences of the early 1980s that would serve him and the family business well. First, he learned the importance of operating from a position of financial strength. While the business has faced challenges since 1984, says Glenn, "We never got backed into a corner that we couldn't get out of." He prides himself that Wenger's has come to be known as a "check writer" that other companies trust and are eager to do business with.

The second lesson Glenn learned was the importance of keeping inventory fresh.

"If you have too much inventory that sits for too long a period of time, it's extremely difficult to make money in this business," says Glenn. After cleaning house in spring 1984, he recalls, "business just went much easier. We had gotten rid of all of our ailments."

Glenn soon would have many opportunities to apply the lessons he was learning. Having exhibited great leadership potential in FFA positions—including service as State FFA Vice-President—22-year-old Glenn was named

---

Neatness Counts

Carl appreciates neatness and order. He admires businesses with fleets of clean, well-maintained trucks. He likes to see his own equipment parked in straight, orderly rows. And he despises noxious weeds and litter. He has spearheaded decades-long crusades against both. On the weed front, thistles are his arch-nemesis.

"Oh, he hates thistles," says son, Lloyd. "He'll get up at 5 o'clock in the morning with a scythe or whatever. He'll go walk about the property and chop down all the thistles."

"He'll even go out in the meadow to get the thistles," adds daughter, Rose. "He doesn't just want the ones along the road."

"And it's not just getting thistles off your own property," says grandson Jake Walmer, recounting a time when his grandpa dragged him out of bed at 5 a.m. to launch a surprise attack on hundreds of thistles in someone else's field along Route 422.

Carl has called in reinforcements from state road crews and ordered them to clean up islands at interchanges, and even a "no man's land" adjacent to an area church.

When he's not fighting thistles, he is waging an equally aggressive campaign against trash. For a number of years Carl posted signs along his properties, proclaiming "Nice People Don't Litter." When not-nice people littered anyway, Carl frequently stopped to pick up trash.

"Dad's fussy with driving around and picking up all the soda cans and the beer bottles," says Lloyd, "something I don't think someone of his age or of his stature should be worried about. It just worries him to death."

Concerned for Carl's safety as he performed rubbish patrol by foot on uneven terrain, his children bought him a golf cart. Despite their best efforts to protect their leader, Carl was wounded in action during a skirmish on King Street. Bending over to retrieve a beer can, Carl accidentally stepped in a hole, twisted his leg, and was evacuated to the hospital for the evening.

He lost that battle, but not his resolve to continue his crusade against trash and noxious weeds.

Carl and Margaret display the fruits of a 2011 trash round-up around their property in Myerstown. They have pledged to let the clean up responsibilities to other "nice people" in the future.

Vice-President and General Manager of the business in 1985, presaging bigger things to come. Though baby-faced Glenn hardly looked old enough to lead a major business, his tender age and youthful appearance belied more than a decade of experience and a natural gift for business. Like his older siblings, and like his father before him, Glenn had grown up in the family business, and was entrusted with and embraced responsibility at an early age.

Eldest brother Lloyd continued as President, but Glenn increasingly was driving the business. "Lloyd was a salesman," explains Glenn. "He wanted to sell. Lloyd never liked the back office stuff. The financing and all that wasn't his thing. And that's where I was coming on."

Youngest daughter, Rose, would graduate from Elizabethtown College in 1986 and, after brief outside employment in social services, would take on Human Resources responsibilities for the company.

With the younger siblings infusing new energy into the business, Wenger's surged during the latter half of the 1980s, moving from financial peril in 1984 to a huge new state-of-the-art facility along Myerstown's major north-south thoroughfare five years later. Seeking to explain the rapid rise after their deliverance from debt, Glenn observes, "We were rejuvenated. I came in at that point, and we were a young group—my brothers and sisters and I—and we had a lot of energy. We were ready to go conquer the world and it just rolled."

They soon decided that it would be easier to conquer the world from a more visible location. Though he hadn't talked with his children about it, Carl often had dreamed of relocating the business from sleepy Race Street to busy Route 501, with its steady stream of traffic. In his mind's eye, he had pictured a horseshoe-shaped complex on the west side of 501—where Wenger's already owned land—with separate wings for the ag equipment and construction equipment divisions.

Instead of moving to the west side of 501, Glenn and his siblings set their sights on a 40-acre tract of land on the east side of the highway, just outside of Myerstown. Glenn first remembers broaching the idea with his older brothers in a bus on the way to a Phillies game. Before long they had their own game plan in place. Carl advised that they move quickly to purchase the land they needed before other potential buyers became involved. They did, and by the summer of 1988 work on a new facility had begun, with brother-in-law Dennis Dieffenbach using his real estate expertise to play a central role.

In November 1988, as the new Wenger's, Inc., building was rising, Glenn invited his siblings and their spouses to go away for a weekend retreat to discuss the future of the business. While

Expensive Education

While Carl has been an advocate of higher education at times through the years, most of the Wenger family received their education through hands-on experience. Youngest daughter Rose Walmer was one of two Wenger children to graduate from Elizabethtown College, and the only college graduate among the siblings to work in the family business. Older sister Carol Dieffenbach graduated from Elizabethtown and chose a career with the Veterans Administration.

Of course, there's more than one way to get an education. Carl and most of his children were schooled on the job and got their education by learning from their mistakes.

"We did some dumb things along the way," explains Glenn, "but that's just education. I never went to college, but I paid more for education than those who go to college to become a doctor."

the Wengers talked business, the spouses went shopping. There was some debate, says Carl, over whether he, as Chairman of the Board, should participate in the meeting, but in the end he honored his children's request to not go along. In retrospect, he believes this was the right decision. "They could never come back and say that Mom and Pop had an influence on where they settled in," Carl explains. "They did that all themselves."

What they did was make official what had already become clear: Glenn would be the one to lead the business. He was named President of the company, and significant areas of responsibility were identified for each of the other siblings. As Glenn remembers it, "There was never a question when we went away for that weekend in 1988 what was going to happen. There wasn't a question in my mind, and I don't think there was a question in anyone else's mind. . . . At that point it was just evident that this would be my role, and they have their roles."

Instead of sibling rivalry and jockeying for position and power, Glenn saw quite the opposite. He perceived his siblings to be thankful and relieved that he felt called to lead the business. While they each had strengths to contribute, says Glenn, "They didn't want to do what I was doing."

His siblings recall it the same way. "It kind of naturally fell to Glenn," says older brother Larry, "and we accepted that. It wasn't a bitter fight or a struggle. We realized we were better doing something else."

Upon their return from retreat, the children reported to Carl and Margaret that Wenger's, Inc., had a new President.

The following year, in March 1989, the agricultural division relocated to its new 60,000-square-foot state of the art facility along Route 501. The building included space for offices; a retail store and parts counter; indoor facilities to tear down tractors and clean and dismantle parts; a football field-size climate controlled warehouse outfitted with enough massive 18-foot-high rack shelving to store tens of thousands of tractor parts from floor to ceiling; and shipping facilities equipped to handle anything from pieces weighing less than an ounce to a diesel engine block tipping the scale at a quarter ton.

A New Era

The new building represented not just new space at a better location, but also huge gains in efficiency and a new era for the business.

In the early years sometimes customers themselves had trudged out behind the barn in the cold of winter or heat of summer to retrieve needed parts—if they were lucky enough to find the right make and model machine. As the salvage business grew, mechanics had haphazardly torn down tractors, often to fill specific parts orders. Various tractors would be partially dismantled until the mechanic got to the needed parts. Equipment in various states of disassembly was shuttled back and forth as new orders needed to be filled, and customers sometimes had to wait a day or more for mechanics to retrieve the needed parts. Some dismantling took place out in the salvage lot and some in the shop.

No more. The new facility brought with it a whole new way of doing business. Instead of haphazardly removing parts as needed or as time allowed, the new facility was designed to streamline the entire process. Now, a tractor could be unloaded from flatbed truck in the morning and by the end of the day have all parts removed, inspected, washed, cataloged, and placed on the warehouse shelf. With a new computerized inventory, customers now could order a part and have it loaded in their truck or readied for shipping within minutes. Clearly, it was a new day for Wenger's, Inc. Over the next decade, some 5,000 tractors would be disassembled in the new facility, building up an inventory of more than 100,000 different parts.

The Wenger fleet of trucks on display in 2007.

Changing Churches

In addition to the major transition taking place at the business, Carl and Margaret made a shift in their personal lives in the latter part of the 1980s, when a misunderstanding with another prominent member spurred them to move from the Midway to the Myerstown Church of the Brethren. Though they had lived just a stone's throw from the Myerstown Church and rubbed shoulders with its members in school and community activities for some four decades, Carl and Margaret had remained active in the church of their youth. But they weren't always in tune with the traditional Midway culture.

During the late 1970s, Carl had questioned positions taken by the church on membership requirements and support of Elizabethtown College. Though Carl in many ways is a staunch conservative, in both disagreements with the church his views were more liberal than the church's.

In a November 9, 1977, letter to the church board (in which he bristled at being required to put his views in writing), Carl wrote, "I find that I am not aware of the goals of this church. From my analysis, I come to realize that it is very hard for a person to become a member of our church and be fully accepted by the members who have been born and raised in a Brethren home."

Though he didn't specifically state it in the letter, the issue he was addressing was Midway's rebaptism requirement for new members transferring their membership from other denominations. The congregation required all new members who had been baptized by means other than immersion to undergo a proper Brethren baptism in order to join the church. Carl felt this was an unreasonable requirement and argued that the church should "open the doors for outsiders" and "be as willing to open our hearts to them as we are the doors."

Carl's interest in the rebaptism issue was more relational than theological. His concern was for close, personal friends in the congregation—the wife a member and the husband unable to join without rebaptism. (Similar scenarios had played out in other Brethren congregations before and following a 1958 Annual Conference decision permitting the acceptance of transferring members on former baptisms. Another three decades would pass before Midway would accept transferring members on their former baptisms.)

Carl continued to advocate for change over the next few years, as evidenced by a May 1979 personal note from friends, expressing appreciation for Carl's "efforts to open minds on the baptism issue." The writer observed, "Like the Pharisees, we all find it easy to take a stand on a legal technicality, but difficult to sincerely change our own peculiar exclusivist attitudes." Of course, the Midway Brethren saw it more as a matter of defending biblical truth.

Another area of concern to Carl was Midway's relationship with Elizabethtown College. In his 1977 letter to the Midway board, Carl expressed dismay at Midway's decision to discontinue financial support of the Church of the Brethren-affiliated college. The church had pulled support due to what it saw as the college leadership's liberal leanings. Carl felt that new college

President Mark C. Ebersole, inaugurated in November 1977, was a solid leader, worthy of the church's support.

"I am . . . very unhappy for the position that our church takes in reference to Elizabethtown College," Carl wrote. He concluded, "I am also aware that we lost interest of members due to the church making such a narrow-minded decision."

Despite these misgivings, Carl and Margaret remained committed to the church at Midway. Carl began serving as Church Treasurer in 1979. And Carl and Margaret and Carl's mother still had a soft spot for the Midway Brethren, as evidenced by their footing the bill for padding on the church pews in 1979.

But when another prominent member of the church questioned Carl's management of church funds in the mid-1980s, it was too much. Feeling falsely accused of wrongdoing, in late 1984 Carl stepped down as Treasurer and walked away, disgruntled, from the church. Efforts by church members to bring about reconciliation were unsuccessful. Carl was convinced the church wasn't big enough for him and his detractor. "We didn't go to church at all for a spell," says Carl. The spell lasted three years.

After licking his wounds, in 1987 Carl arranged a lunch meeting with Pastors Glen Hassinger and John Harpold, of Myerstown and Midway, respectively, to clear the air and move on. Before he would join at Myerstown, Carl wanted Midway to fully exonerate him. Resulting from that meeting was a letter, dated November 20, 1987, in which Pastor Harpold assured Carl that the Midway Church held no ill will toward him.

Quoting from a July 14, 1987, board action, Harpold wrote, "By unanimous vote, the Board expressed appreciation for your years of service to the church as Treasurer and in many other ways. The board affirms your integrity noting that there was never any mis-use or mis-direction of Church Funds and that all auditors' reports confirm your complete honesty and proper distribution of Church Funds."

The letter continued, "The desire of the Board is that we may continue in fellowship together and that the past may be laid to rest and that we may move forward in mutual service in the Lord."

Satisfied that he had been exonerated, Carl and Margaret began worshipping at Myerstown—where many of their children and grandchildren already had been attending—and were received as members on November 19, 1989. He returned to Midway once a year to worship with his mother on Mother's Day until her death in 1994.

Carl says today he has nothing but good feelings toward the Midway Church, where son Larry serves as an elder. When Midway added a $375,000 educational wing in 1995, Carl and Margaret gave a generous donation in honor of his mother, who had taught Sunday school for many years. His relationship with the individual member who he felt wronged him, however, remained cool from that time forward.

1990s Dawning

As the 1990s dawned, Carl and Margaret had a new church and Wenger's, Inc., had a new location, leadership structure, and lease on life. A decade that had begun with the business mired in debt and Carl, himself, deep in depression ended with a thriving business in a state-of-the-art facility. Carl's children were energetic and eager to build on the foundation that he had established. The stage was set for explosive growth during the 1990s that would involve construction of additional facilities, extending the company's reach internationally, launching new initiatives, and acquiring additional affiliates.

The success of the business, however, would be tempered by a family tragedy. That tragedy, in turn, would be transformed into an outpouring of giving and contribute to a shift in focus for Carl from making money to giving it away.

10

Beginnings and Endings

The 1990s represented a number of beginnings and endings for Carl, his family, and the business that he began. Beginnings would include new acquisitions, a new construction equipment facility on the opposite side of Route 501 to match the sprawling agricultural facility, the introduction of a unique breed of cattle to the Wenger farm, a new name for the business, and the creation of a foundation to serve as the charitable giving arm of the Wenger family of companies. Endings would include Carl and Margaret's ownership share in the business and, tragically, the life of a beloved granddaughter and her unborn child.

Growth by Acquisition

Situated in a sparkling new facility with an energetic leadership team in place, Wenger's, Inc., was poised for growth. Their new facility, streamlined processes, and computerization enabled them to increase the parts portion of the business, carrying parts from an ever wider range of makes and models of tractors and machinery and expanding their service area.

The company also was ready to grow by acquiring other businesses. During the early decades, Carl had liquidated a number of smaller equipment dealers and added their inventory to his own. And Wenger's from time to time had sold some lines

Reading Kubota, pictured here in a recent photo, was added to the Wenger Family of Companies in 1993.

of new equipment along with their main line of used equipment and parts. But during the 1990s Wenger's began to grow by adding affiliates to their family of companies—affiliates that specialized in new, rather than used, items.

With Glenn and Carl working together to orchestrate deals, in 1993 they acquired Reading-area Kubota dealer Nicarry Equipment, which they later renamed Reading Kubota. The following year Ag Industrial was added to the Wenger family of companies. Located in Rising Sun, Maryland, Ag Industrial was a New Holland tractor and equipment dealership that specialized in agricultural, light industrial, commercial, and grounds care and turf equipment. (Wenger's would open a new Ag Industrial location in Douglassville, Pennsylvania, in fall 2007, and add a third in New Holland, Pennsylvania, in May 2010 through the acquisition of an existing New Holland dealership.) The new affiliates swelled Wenger's sales volume and increased overall profitability.

As the company was growing through acquiring other businesses during the mid-1990s, the Wengers also were making plans to continue growth at home in Myerstown. In 1996 the company completed a 44,000-square-foot construction parts dealership and warehouse to match the ag division across Route 501. Now the thousands of vehicles daily entering Myerstown from the south would be greeted by a sprawling display of farm equipment on the right side of the road and an equally impressive array of construction equipment on the left. Along with the new facility came growth in the construction equipment parts business, with expansion into the international market, importing and exporting parts and equipment worldwide.

Also in 1996, Wenger's would distribute its first ever parts catalog, with a print run of 60,000. In May 2000 the company reached another landmark when they listed the parts for a Farmall Cub on their website, initiating online parts sales. "We've been working at it ever since," says Larry, who heads the tractor parts department, "still putting more tractors and skid loaders out on the website."

By 2012, says Larry, the Wenger ag parts inventory totaled over a million parts, with 150,000 different part numbers. Of those, 53,000 part numbers from more than 500 tractor and skid loader models were available online, with more being added daily. Across Route 501, parts from larger, more unwieldy construction equipment were being added to inventory at a much slower pace, but today customers from around the world can order from Wenger's extensive parts inventory through an online ordering system that puts needed parts just a few clicks away.

The name of the company was changed to Wengers of Myerstown in 1996 to reflect a broadening scope, and the business began using the phrase "the Wenger family of companies" to describe its expanding footprint.

Despite its rapid growth, the business remained a family affair. With Glenn at the helm, in 1997 Lloyd headed the wholesale construction equipment; Larry and his wife, Becky, the farm tractor parts; and David, retail equipment sales in the ag division. Carl continued as Board Chairman; Nancy oversaw shipping of ag parts; Rose led the recently-formed Wenger Foundation, Inc., and headed Human Resources; and Margaret and daughter Carol joined the rest of the family as directors of the corporation. Some spouses and unrelated employees held other key posts.

In recognition of Glenn's role in the company's accomplishments, the Lebanon Valley Chamber of Commerce awarded him its 1996 "Small Business Person of the Year Award." The company would add a machine shop in 2002 and a used motorcycle sales division in January 2006. A fledgling engine rebuilding operation got underway in April 2011. Along the way, not everything was successful. An affiliate in Florida closed after several years, and new trailer sales begun in Myerstown in 2005 proved unprofitable.

Meanwhile, Down on the Farm

While the center of activity for Wenger's during the 1990s was shifting to the new facilities along Route 501, the business still included an operating farm back on Race Street, with its lush pasture land along the Tulpehocken Creek. In 1994 the Wengers populated those pastures with an ancient breed of cattle that would put the farming portion of the business on the map.

Until 1980 Wenger's had operated several dairy farms, but by the mid-1990s they raised just a few Holstein heifers on the home farm. Glenn, who says he inherited his grandfather's cattle gene, thought it would be nice to have some calves on the farm again. His mother agreed. When Margaret pointed out an article in *Lancaster Farming* about unusual American British White Park Cattle, Glenn was intrigued. "I wanted something different and unique," he recalls. White Park Cattle fit the bill.

He returned from auctions in Indiana and Missouri in 1994 with a bull and nine heifers.

"As far as I know," says Glenn, "Wengers were the first ones in Pennsylvania to have registered White Park Cattle." Today, says Glenn, as many as 20 farms in Pennsylvania raise White Parks, many of whom got their start with stock from the Wenger herd. While not officially classified as a rare breed, the majority

A Noble History

Lean and rugged White Park Cattle—named for their color and the estates in England that they inhabited—are thought to have roamed wild for hundreds of years, dating back nearly to the time of Christ, when Roman legions occupied the British Isles. During the 12th and 13th centuries, land in England was distributed by Norman occupiers to nobility, with estates separated by high fences and stone walls to form "parks." The "emparked" cattle continued to live wild and natural selection continued to strengthen the breed.

According to a breeder's association website, "The cattle that survived in each generation were superior. . . . The basic qualities of hardiness, livability, disease resistance, fertility and feed efficiency enabled a part of each generation to survive and reproduce themselves. These basic traits of functional efficiency became more bred-in and more firmly established with each succeeding generation."

Eventually, the cattle were domesticated and breeders began to build on their inherent strengths. In 1940, one bull and five cows were sent to the United States to be used as seed stock in event of a Nazi invasion of England. Nearly all White Park Cattle in the U.S. trace their bloodlines to this one shipment. In about 1960 all park cattle in the custody of the U.S. government were sold to the public. A breeder's association was formed in 1975, eventually evolving into the American British White Park Association.

American British White Park Cattle are recognized for their beauty and quality at home on the Wenger farm and in competitions, like this Reserve Champion Bull at the 2011 Keystone International Livestock Exposition in Quincy, Illinois (above). The bull is flanked by Glenn Wenger (left) and herdsman Bill Paul.

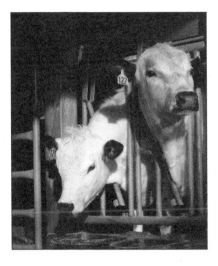

white cattle with patches of black and brown, are uncommon in the United States.

Wengers began showing their cattle in 1999 and, according to a fall 2008 sale bill, from 2000 to 2007 they earned 30 Champion and Reserve Champion titles, including 10 national titles. The large majority of awards were earned at the Keystone International Livestock Exposition, held each fall in Harrisburg, Pennsylvania, and billed as the largest livestock show in the eastern United States. Other competitions included the World Beef Expo in Milwaukee, Wisconsin, and the Annual National American British White Parks Show held at the Adams County Fair in Quincy, Illinois.

Glenn eventually became president of the national American British White Park Association, and for the past several years has served as interim Executive Secretary of the 180-member organization.

Today Carl and Margaret can look out their windows and see a herd of some 65 contented White Park Cattle—35 cows plus bulls and young stock—grazing in the meadow along Race Street. "Mother loves to see them in the pasture," says Glenn.

Shady Grove Village

While handsome white cattle grazed peacefully in the meadow at Myerstown, Carl persisted in seeking out greener pastures for his business. He continued to enjoy his regular rounds at equipment auctions in the South, through which he had established many friendships over the years. He came to the aid of one of those friends when a series of unfortunate events threatened ruin.

Over the years Carl had developed a friendship and business relationship with Ron and Hilda Schuler, owners of a 400-tree pecan farm and a farm machinery business near Cairo, Georgia. Carl and Ron crossed paths frequently at Weeks Auction Company in Moultrie, Georgia, sometimes purchasing and re-selling equipment together and sharing the profits.

When three hurricanes swept through Georgia in close succession in 1985, the Schulers' pecan crop was devastated, placing them in dire financial straits. With bank foreclosure looming over the Schulers' 60-acre farm, Carl intervened on behalf of his friends.

Over time Carl and the Schulers made plans to develop a portion of the farm into a 40-plot subdivision. Shady Grove Village, as it is called, opened for business in January 1996, marketing 34 half-acre lots and several larger ones for placement of multi-unit manufactured homes.

Four years later, wracked by an incurable form of cancer, Ron Schuler escaped his suffering by ending his life. Again Carl and Margaret were there. Carl bought the Schulers' share of the subdivision, set Hilda up with a free home to live in for life, and employed her to manage the affairs of the development.

Soon after assuming responsibility for Shady Grove Village, Carl mixed business with pleasure in a benefit event. Partnering with other area businesses, he spearheaded an open house and benefit concert at the village to benefit the family of an area builder, named Smith, who had suffered serious injuries in a car accident. The event featured food, door prizes, and Southern Gospel music. Participants gave nearly $5,000 to benefit the Smith family. In a *Cairo Messenger* article,

Mrs. Smith pledged to give 10 percent back to the Wenger Foundation, and share another 10 percent with a young girl in need in the community.

In typical Carl Wenger fashion, the event blended a business aspect, food, gospel music, and an opportunity for others to join him in supporting a worthy cause.

Several years earlier, Carl had responded to a tragedy in his own family with an event on a much larger scale.

A Family Tragedy

On August 13, 1994, the Wenger family was rocked by the murder of Carl and Margaret's 19-year-old granddaughter Renee Ann Layser. The middle daughter of Carl's daughter, Nancy, and her husband, John Layser, Renee had become a Christian and joined the Myerstown Church of the Brethren at age 13. After a stint as a part-time secretary-receptionist at Wenger's, Renee took a job as a bank teller.

In early 1994, she made a bad choice to become involved with a young man. A few months later she confessed to her parents that she was pregnant, but resolved to choose life for her child and began to prepare for motherhood. Although the circumstances surrounding her pregnancy were difficult, the Wenger family rallied around Renee and supported her in her decision to parent her child. Unfortunately, the father of her child did not.

He pressured Renee to have an abortion. An argument over potential child support escalated, and he killed his former girlfriend. The killer eventually confessed and in March 1995 received a life sentence for the murder. Renee was 23 weeks into her pregnancy when she was killed.

The tragic loss of Renee and her unborn child was a huge blow to her parents, grandparents, and extended family that would weigh heavily on the Layser and Wenger families for years to come. But Carl's response was to try to bring something good out of the evil that had taken place.

Carl and Margaret's first response was to give a major gift in Renee's memory to support disaster relief. They donated a quilt to the 1994 Brethren Disaster Relief Auction, which was held several weeks after Renee's death. Carl and Margaret had purchased the quilt, crafted by women of the Myerstown Church, at a previous disaster auction.

Bids for the memorial quilt climbed steadily as people were

In 1994 the Wenger family was rocked by the murder of Carl and Margaret's granddaughter, Renee, shown here in her high school senior picture.

touched by the tragic story. In the end Carl and Margaret bought it back and gave it to Renee's sister, Greta, as a wedding gift. Their $10,450 bid was the second highest ever given for a quilt at the auction (bested only by a quilt crafted by 100-year-old Lizzie Longenecker, purchased by her son, Carl, in 1989 for $10,600).

But Carl wasn't done honoring the memory of his granddaughter. He had bigger plans. For more than a decade, he had envisioned starting a Foundation for charitable giving, but had not seen his dream realized. "I wanted a Foundation for 10 to 15 years before it ever got started," Carl says. "They always told me that I didn't have enough of backing. The accountants and the attorneys were all squeamish."

At the same time, he had had some initial conversations with friends about sponsoring local Southern Gospel concerts to raise funds for worthy causes. Now, following Renee's death, people were wondering what they could do to express their sympathy for the Wenger family. And Carl told them: They could attend a $100-a-plate dinner, enjoy some Southern Gospel music, and have their gifts channeled through a new foundation to support a worthy cause.

Son Glenn initiated the legal work to create the Wenger Foundation, Inc., and daughter Rose spearheaded plans for a Memorial Dinner. Checks started coming in, made out to the Wenger Foundation even before the foundation officially existed, Carl recalls. "We had faith that Glenn would get his job done."

Carl invited planners of the Brethren Disaster Relief Auction to help sponsor the event, but because of the circumstances surrounding Renee's death, they were reluctant to fully embrace the dinner. Auction Coordinators Mel and Gloria Burkholder, however, joined hands with the Wengers to personally co-sponsor the event, with proceeds benefitting the auction.

Held May 2, 1996, at the Lebanon Expo Center, the Renee A. Layser Memorial Dinner attracted nearly 800 people. The program included a buffet dinner; entertainment by The Anchormen, Christian comedy ventriloquist act Geraldine and Rickey, and soloist Kirk Talley; and a mini-auction. Auctioned during intermission were a peacock quilt made by women of the Myerstown Church, two carved paintings by artist Abner Zook, and some Longaberger Baskets. (Renee had been a Longaberger sales consultant and had an eye for their baskets.) Glenn emceed the event and served as auctioneer. Among the event's highlights was Talley's rendition of "Serenaded by Angels" and a concluding candlelight memorial in Renee's honor.

The writer of an article in the 1996 *Disaster Auction Sale Book* summed up: "This event was a wonderful way to share our love for Renee and to show other (sic) how the Lord can reach out to us even during our deepest times of sorrow. This event was truly a celebration of life."

Some of Carl's friends wondered whether he had gone over the edge when he pronounced a $100,000 fundraising goal

Nearly 800 people attended the Renee A. Layser Memorial Dinner in 1996. The event raised $110,000 for the Church of the Brethren Emergency Disaster Fund. Photo by Daniel Culhane.

for the dinner, but final results proved his sanity. At the end of the evening donations and mini-auction proceeds totaled $110,000.

Praise Dinners

With the Foundation and formula established, the Wengers—with support from the Burkholders and Donald and Francis Layser—planned a second dinner the following year, now known as the Wenger Foundation Praise Dinner. This time the event attracted 450 people and raised $45,000 for the BDRA.

In 1998, Carl sought to broaden the base of support for the event by splitting proceeds between disaster relief and Lebanon Valley Youth for Christ. Attendance and support disappointingly dropped by more than 25 percent. The downward trend was reversed in 1999 with the inclusion of COBYS Family Services and Evangelical School of Theology (later renamed Evangelical

Carl is in his element at the annual Wenger Foundation Praise Dinner. He is shown here (left) greeting guest Sheryl Faus at the 2004 Praise Dinner and holding court with State FFA officers at the 2001 event. FFA officers help with some of the heavy lifting for the dinner each year.

Praise Dinner Proceeds

Since its inception in 1996, the Wenger Foundation Praise Dinner has generated more than a million dollars to support these ministries:

Brethren Disaster Relief Auction	$230,262
COBYS Family Services	242,306
Evangelical Seminary	194,976
Friendship Community	238,037
Lebanon Valley Youth for Christ	12,802
On-Fire Youth Ministry	247,951
Total	$1,166,334

Seminary) as beneficiaries. Donors also were able to designate their contributions for the first time. Friendship Community was added as a beneficiary the following year.

Since 2003, the annual Praise Dinner has benefitted COBYS, Evangelical Seminary, Friendship Community, and On-Fire Youth Ministries of Myerstown.

Throughout its history the Praise Dinner formula has changed little: Plan a $100-a-plate dinner featuring a great meal and nationally known Southern Gospel groups and speakers. Cover all costs of the event with generous support from Carl and Margaret, the Wenger family, and other business sponsors. Invite businesses to sponsor tables and businesses and individuals to give to the ministry of their choice. Enjoy an evening of food and upbeat Christian entertainment. Celebrate the outpouring of giving.

The Praise Dinner bears Carl's unique stamp, bringing together several of his interests and embodying his philosophy of giving. In the early years, the event dovetailed with Carl's interest in the Brethren Disaster Relief Auction, channeling significant support to assist victims of disasters. In more recent years, Carl's lifelong interest in FFA has been on display as state FFA officers, sporting their signature blue jackets, have assisted in setting up and tearing down tables and chairs at the Praise Dinner. Carl's love of good food and Southern Gospel music also find expression at the event.

When it comes to philanthropy, Carl likes to give in ways that inspire others to join him. While Carl gives generously, himself, to underwrite the costs of the dinner, much of the event's success is owed to the many other businesses and individuals who join hands with Carl and the Foundation. The results have been astounding. At the 15th annual Praise Dinner in April 2010, total giving for the life of the event eclipsed the million dollar mark. Including the 2011 Praise Dinner, total giving now stands at $1,166,334.

In addition, the Foundation channels corporate donations from the Wenger family of companies and individual contributions from Carl and Margaret and their seven children and families to a variety of community and Christian causes. All told, since its inception the Foundation has donated more than $1.89 million to some 150 organizations.

Fetal Homicide Law

As a result of Renee's death, the Layser and Wenger families also advocated in behalf of state fetal homicide legislation. An August 1994 *Reading Eagle* article explained:

> John Layser had expected to feel a sense of closure when a Berks County jury convicted his daughter's killer of first-degree murder after a 10-day trial in March 1995.
>
> But while Jeffrey Clapsadl would spend the rest of his life in prison, Layser felt justice had not been served. His daughter was five months pregnant by Clapsadl, her ex-boyfriend, when he killed her with a shotgun blast to the head.
>
> Clapsadl had told her not to have the baby. But Renee Layser, 19, had been eagerly awaiting motherhood. She read baby books and kept a little chest in her room with baby clothes and bottles. John Layser and his wife, Nancy, were planning a baby shower for their first grandchild.
>
> Pennsylvania courts have long held that no criminal charges can be brought in the death of a fetus, but the Lebanon County family [Laysers] wanted recognition for that loss as well. So this year, they turned to State Sen. Edward W. Helfrick (R., Northumberland), whose antiabortion views are well-known.

As a result, a fetal homicide bill—which would make it a crime to kill or seriously injure an unborn child intentionally or recklessly—is now on the verge of becoming law.

Later in 1997, Governor Tom Ridge signed legislation into law defining the killing of an unborn child as homicide and stipulating punishment up to life imprisonment for a person who "intentionally, knowingly, recklessly or negligently causes the death of an unborn child." Since then the legislation has been amended and survived court challenges from pro-abortion forces.

The tragic death of a granddaughter and her unborn child was transformed, giving birth to a Foundation that has been a blessing to dozens of organizations and thousands of people and legislation that recognizes the value of unborn children. "Her life was not in vain," says Carl, "although she is greatly missed."

A Celebration to Remember

As the calendar turned to 1997, a big birthday loomed on the horizon for Carl. On his 35th birthday in 1967 he had borrowed a half million dollars to keep his business afloat. For his 65th, he wanted to do something really big to celebrate not only his birthday, but the ultimate success of his business. "I wanted to have something that nobody else had in our area," he explained.

What he ended up having was an all-day event at the Lebanon Expo Center on Saturday, November 22, to simultaneously celebrate his 65th birthday and the 50th anniversary of Wenger's of Myerstown. To make it all work, the party had to wait until six months after his actual May 20 birthday, and he had to fudge a little on the start date of the business.

"Hey, when people ask me about the start of the business," Carl explains, "I don't know what to tell them. You know, I started when I was 12 years old [as nickel man at his Uncle's sale]. You can take that as a start. You can take when I got married and took over the farm in '51 as the start. Or you can take when we incorporated Wenger's in '57. You can take anything you want to take and you wouldn't be far off."

Carl took 1947, because it made his 65th birthday coincide with the 50th anniversary of the business. It wasn't far off, but he does remember banker friend Leonard Schott giving him a hard time that Wenger's already had celebrated a 50th anniversary a few years earlier.

Not wanting to miss anyone, Carl took out newspaper ads and posted signs inviting friends, family members, and customers of the Wenger family of companies to join him for "Wenger Celebration Day" at the Lebanon Expo Center. (He did send out a few invitations, including one to Governor Tom Ridge. The Governor and First Lady sent their regrets through a letter from his Chief of Staff.)

Built around a country fair theme, the all-day event featured live musical performances from the Frank DiNunzio Orchestra, The Nottingham Four, and the Rajah Chanters; exhibits of various Wengers of Myerstown divisions and affiliates and a new promotional video; displays from other area businesses; and, of course, generous portions of free food, including a truckload of Kauffman's chicken, scrumptious beef from one of the Wengers' own White Park steers, and a huge birthday cake and ice cream.

Displays from Wengers of Myerstown, Reading Kubota, and Ag Industrial anchored the corners of the main exhibit hall and a Wenger truck with flatbed trailer served as a stage for the entertainment. The construction division was represented by two excavators at the entrance with buckets raised high to form an archway for partygoers to pass through as they entered the grounds. Prizes were awarded to the people who brought along the oldest Wenger's invoice and oldest piece of Wenger's memorabilia.

As part of the celebration, Carl was inducted as an honorary member of the Myerstown Rotary Club. As an honorary member, he didn't face the same weekly attendance requirements as a full member, but he quickly embraced the work of Rotary and continues his involvement today.

Former FFA instructor and longtime family friend Gerald Strickler made arrangements with the *Lebanon Daily News* to publish a 16-page tabloid the day before the big celebration. It featured a half dozen stories on Carl's life, various aspects of the business, and the fledgling Wenger Foundation, along with many family- and business-related photos and ads from more than 50 businesses. Fifteen years later Carl still carries a copy with him to familiarize people with the Wenger story.

An estimated 1,000 people came out for the memorable celebration, with each family unit receiving a goody bag of promotional items. Instead of bringing personal gifts for Carl, he invited guests to contribute to the Wenger Foundation in his honor, which they did to the tune of $7,000. While the giving was generous, it was far less than it cost Carl to host the party.

Bought Out

With Carl having turned 65 in May 1997, his children decided it was time to complete the transfer of the business to the next generation—a process that had begun three decades earlier. In November 1967, Carl's father had divided his share of the business into nine equal shares for Carl, Margaret, and each of their children. As a result, all of the children had an ownership stake in the business, including the two youngest children, who had yet to enter school.

*This photo of Wengers of Myerstown's Board of Directors appeared in
a tabloid printed in conjunction with the 1997 Wenger Celebration Day.
Pictured with Carl and Margaret are (standing from left) daughters Carol
Dieffenbach, Rose Walmer, and Nancy Layser.*

The process of transferring the business continued a number of years later, when the children's non-voting stock was
converted to voting stock. By the 1990s the next generation
was essentially running the business, with Glenn serving as
President and other siblings and their spouses serving in primary leadership roles. But Carl remained actively engaged, serving as Chairman of the Board, and he and Margaret still owned
more than half of the business. But that was about to change.

"They wanted to know if I would sell the rest to them,"
says Carl, "and I said, 'Give me a deal.' They went and got fair
numbers and they figured it out and I took their deal. They were
taught to do fair business."

The process of determining fair value for the business and negotiating among children how to affect their portion of the transfer was a bit more complex than that—not all children chose to buy their one-seventh of the stock—but as of January 1, 1998, Carl no longer had an ownership stake in the business to which he had dedicated his life.

Reflecting back on the transaction, Glenn remembers buying out his parents as "just a natural progression. . . . It just was the natural flow of things. There's no watershed moment."

At the same time, Glenn acknowledges that Wengers of Myerstown had successfully cleared a hurdle fraught with potential for misunderstanding and conflict. While many family businesses flounder at the point of transfer, creating bad blood and even severing relationships, the Wengers completed the complicated transfer of the family business to the next generation with both the business and family ties in tact. And close family ties persist.

"We've always had a lot of respect for our parents and that has really held the family together," says Lloyd. "My generation has a lot of respect for our parents and we would not do anything to hurt them."

Glenn cites a couple factors that contributed to the successful transition and harmonious working relationships: Siblings who live within their means and don't feel a sense of entitlement and spouses who have been content to let family members manage the business.

"I never had a brother or sister or myself feel entitled to anything," says Glenn. "We all live comfortable lifestyles, but none of us ever lived above our means." The result has been a lack of questioning each other's motives and anger and resentment over squandering the business's—and family's—resources.

And while spouses work for the company and carry important roles, says Glenn, with few exceptions they have been content to let the Wenger siblings set the direction and manage the business's affairs.

"We just have been extremely fortunate," says Glenn, "that none of the seven spouses have ever felt the need to put their nose in and have a say in how we decide to run this business."

Undergirding everything is a deep trust that Carl and Margaret's children share.

"The bond that exists between my brothers and sisters," says Glenn, "is almost unexplainable. There is nothing that I wouldn't do for a brother or sister. We all trust each other and none of the seven of us has ever violated that trust. I can't explain it, but I believe it to be truly uncommon."

Larry gives his father some credit for setting the business up in such a way that it could succeed: "Dad was wise enough to set the business up that we weren't that close that we were butting heads," Larry observes. "We all work for the same business, but we each have our own niche or department. We're far enough apart that we're not fighting each other."

"We all can make the final decision for our area of responsibility," adds Davey. "We don't have to go to somebody to say, 'Is it okay to do this or okay to do that?'" And, he adds, "If you make a wrong decision, that's your baby. Deal with it. Straighten it out."

"That's a lot of it," agrees Lloyd. "We don't have a lot of people stepping on toes all the time. It's big enough we all can go our own way."

By the Numbers

The company that Carl's offspring purchased from Carl at the end of 1997 was a very different company from the one that Carl began—or even the one that new President Glenn Wenger took charge of in 1988. Fueled by acquisitions and growth at home, annual business volume during the decade from 1988 to 1997 tripled to an estimated $23 million. The company employed

Equipment on display at the main ag facility along Route 501 in Myerstown today.

66 people, 57 of them full-time, and carried a computerized inventory of some 200,000 agricultural and construction equipment parts. Workers daily added to that number, disassembling 40 tractors per month, along with additional pieces of construction equipment. A February 2006 *Lebanon Daily News* article reported that the company had dismantled more than 6,500 tractors within the previous 20 years.

Larry Wenger, who was instrumental in computerized and managing the ag parts, observed in 1997, "We have the largest inventory of its type, in a heated warehouse with a computer inventory." Agricultural business at that time was anchored in the mid-Atlantic region, but extended into the Midwest and other parts of the country. The construction parts division, housed in its new facility, was serving companies doing business in places as far afield as the Middle East, Malaysia, and South America, according to Lloyd.

A local Lebanon County business that Carl Wenger began with a half dozen manure spreaders parked behind the barn had been built into a multi-million dollar company with customers across the country and halfway around the globe.

Since the time his children became part-owners of the business in 1967, Carl had always claimed that they weren't working for him; he was working for them. Now, 30 years later, it was literally true. Carl would maintain an office, continue to buy and sell, and remain an ambassador for the business. He relishes opportunities to provide tours of Wengers of Myerstown's impressive facilities and tell the story of the company that he founded. But the business now belonged to the next generation. And Carl wasn't even on the payroll.

Looking back on his accomplishments, Carl Wenger had much to be proud of and was pleased to see that his life's work was now in the competent hands of his offspring. But he wasn't ready just yet to rest on his laurels.

11

Not Really Retired

As the turn of a new century approached, life was good for Carl and Margaret. For eight months out of the year they continued to live in Myerstown, with all seven children and their families living close by. During the winter months they set up housekeeping in their comfortable Florida home.

While Carl no longer had an ownership stake in Wengers of Myerstown, his involvement in the business and drive to see it succeed was scarcely diminished. And he was by no means retired. At the dawn of a new year in 1998, he established new goals and resolved to add enough value to the company over the next few years to match the installment payments he would be receiving from his children for the buyout.

To track his progress, the company set up a Southern Division and turned Carl loose. Attending sales from his home base in Florida, Carl did what he had always done best—buying and selling tractors and equipment for a profit. He developed an expanded network of dealers and a thriving wholesale business. As Glenn remembers it, over the next four or five years Carl succeeded in single-handedly generating annual profits of $200,000 or more for the business, meeting his ambitious goal of essentially paying himself off for the business.

A Day at an Auction

In an unpublished manuscript written in 1997, Richard Anglestein described how Carl meticulously prepared for and worked an auction in the south one oppressively hot day during the latter half of 1990s:

Days before a big auction, Carl will start working on the telephones to get tentative ideas of the equipment needs of potential retail customers. Other family members who work daily in the selling of the parts are consulted on what makes and models are in demand or are needed to replace depleted inventory. He doesn't wait until auction day to take his first steps on the bidding field. As soon as the equipment is aligned in its rows, Carl may be found walking the lines. He stops at each piece, examines it closely, and jots down extensive notes.

The notes would include make, model, serial number, hours, and observations on the condition of each piece. Then drawing on his vast experience and factoring in what his current customers were looking for, he would determine how high he would be willing to go on each piece when the bidding would begin the next day.

Carl's meticulous records and bulging shirt pocket made a lasting impression on Grady Weeks, from Weeks Auction Company, in Ocala, Florida, where Carl has been a regular buyer. "He always carried a three-inch-thick stack of cards in his shirt pocket," wrote Grady (perhaps exaggerating a bit), "containing all types of information concerning tractors and equipment. He always knew the value of equipment because he not only carried the cards, he studied them."

Of course, one downside of Carl's meticulous record keeping and shirt pocket filing system was that Margaret constantly was called upon to sew torn shirt pockets that had one—or maybe one hundred—too many note cards stuffed into them.

Anglestein continues with his account of a Florida auction:

Dinner the night before a sale is not one of idle chatter. Carl is already conducting tomorrow's sale and checking details with dinner partners. The morning of a sale begins very early by calling last minute potential customers, giving each an exact rundown of details of equipment in which they may be interested, and a last minute call home checks for any salvage parts that may be needed. Finally, it's off to the sale—a sale that actually began days ago in Carl's mind. One final stop to stock the van's cooler with ice and plenty of cold sodas for the day.

Clad in cowboy boots and hat, and sporting the "W" on his belt buckle, Carl followed the auction trailer down the row of tractors, buying more than his fair share, each with a rap of a gavel and a cry of "Sold—Wengers of Myerstown!"

His stocky figure is so well known that auctioneers constantly keep him within their sweeping gaze. An almost imperceptible bob of the hat, which almost goes unnoticed by the crowd, heads another tractor to Pennsylvania.

As the sun sank lower in the sky, there were three or four flat-bed trucks to load with the day's purchases, more phone calls to report what equipment was on the way, and preparations to return home, before heading off to another auction in another state.

But even then, Carl wasn't finished. He admits that he often replayed the events of an auction afterwards.

"I go over that whole auction in my mind and see if I made mistakes," he explains. "The mistakes usually are not what you buy, but the pieces that you didn't buy. Then you left something on the table."

More than once Carl would kick himself for missing out on potential profit. "One of the things that made me successful," he says, "was being hard on myself."

A Basketful of Thanks

Soon after they sold out of the business in 1998, Carl and Margaret initiated an unusual collection. It began innocently enough with a hand-written thank you note tossed, almost thoughtlessly, into a basket. But over time it grew into an intentional effort to preserve a record of uncommon thoughtfulness and generosity.

"We have a big basket in the living room," explains Carl, "and we get [notes] and I make sure they have what year on them and I throw them in that basket. I never throw a thank you note away. When I don't get thank you notes, I know I'm not doing enough."

By December 2011, Carl and Margaret had amassed a haphazard collection of more than 900 notes—an average of about 70 per year (although they certainly received more in later years than in early years)—chronicling more than a decade of generosity. (And the basket contained only personal thank yous, not the many official acknowledgments received from the dozens of charities they support.)

The basket contains notes from grandchildren, addressed to Mama and Papa, thanking Carl and Margaret for birthday gifts, graduation presents, and household furnishings.

It includes many thank yous for flowers sent at times of loss, visits and attendance at special birthday and anniversary gatherings, and other expressions of love and thoughtfulness at important times in people's lives.

It contains notes from bank tellers, race track employees, staff at medical and dental offices, and other businesses Carl frequents, thanking him for pretzels, cookies, and other small gifts that Carl dropped off in his travels.

It includes dozens of notes from friends, thanking the Wengers for a good meal and fellowship, or lodging in their Florida home. Many people have enjoyed Carl and Margaret's gracious hospitality, and few have ever eaten with Carl without him paying the bill.

It even includes a few notes from people who unexpectedly had their bills paid, when Carl spied them across the way and quietly picked up their tab, like one from Tessie O.: "Thank you for the breakfast. I went to pay and she said it's taken care of." Carl admits that paying restaurant bills for friends is one of his favorite tricks: "I like to go to the diner and when I see somebody in there who I know, I get the waitress to give me the bill. I pay it, and then I get out of there before they find out."

When Life Gives You Lemons... Eat Them

Nearly everyone is familiar with the old saying, "When life gives you lemons, make lemonade." But Carl has a different take on the sour fruit. When life gives him lemons, he eats them. Anyone who has dined out with Carl in one of his regular haunts knows two things: 1) He probably will pay the bill; and 2) The server will place a small dishful of lemon sections at his spot on the table. He need not ask for lemons. They know.

They also know that they won't have to clear away the rinds after the meal. That's because Carl first squeezes the lemon juice into his tea or water. Then he sorts out the stray seeds. And finally—with nary a pucker—one by one he pops those succulent lemon sections into his mouth, chews thoroughly, and swallows, rind and all.

The lemon ritual is something Carl says he picked up from his father, who also had a sour tooth. Which brings us to a variation on another old adage: "The lemon doesn't fall far from the tree."

Sometimes Carl even picks up the bill for complete strangers who catch his eye. Like the 52-voice Christian youth choir he encountered at McDonalds on his way to Florida in December 2008. He began a conversation with the group's leaders, liked what he heard, and by the time it was all over, Carl had paid their entire bill. "It was a great feeling," he recalls. "The timing was right, the thing was right. It just fit."

Carl's basket includes thank yous from political figures—local, state, and national, in Florida and Pennsylvania, all Republicans—thanking Carl for campaign donations.

In that basket are many thank yous for tickets to concerts, dinners, and other fundraiser events that Carl purchased to benefit various organizations and then passed on to others to enjoy. Included are many expressions of thanks from people who enjoyed the good food and music at Carl's signature event—the

Carl has been a supporter of Republican politicians from the local to the national level. He is shown here in 2010 with former Speaker of the House Newt Gingrich at a Republican fundraising event in Harrisburg.

Lloyd's Toys

Wengers of Myerstown always has a lot of tractors and implements on hand, but their hundreds of pieces of life-size equipment pales in comparison to Lloyd Wenger's toy collection. Lloyd began collecting toys some 40 years ago and now owns what he believes is the largest collection of pedal tractors in the world. In addition, he has amassed thousands of smaller toy tractors, trucks, and farm equipment replicas made by companies like Tonka and Ertl; thousands of sales brochures for various makes and models of tractors; and an unusual collection of farm equipment-related signs. His collection grew so big that twice he has had to build garages to house it, the second one big enough for four bays and high enough for a second floor. Wife, Kitty, has since laid down the law: No more garages. And Lloyd gradually is reducing the size of his collection through eBay sales and occasional shows. But the toy collection remains a must see part of the Wenger tours that Carl enjoys giving to friends and acquaintances.

Wenger Foundation Praise Dinner—and from the widows that Carl and Margaret take as guests each year to the Lebanon Valley Brethren Home Good Samaritan Dinner.

There are thank yous for use of the Wenger cabin and for tours of the Wenger enterprises, which always include son Lloyd's toy collection.

The basket contains many notes from Christian and community ministries, churches, pastors, missionaries, young people going on mission trips, all thanking Carl and Margaret for their gifts and support.

Carl and Margaret have been generous in extending use of their cabin to others, although much of the work to prepare for groups fell to Margaret. Tired of the extra effort, Margaret once facetiously pledged that on her way home from Carl's funeral she would stop at the cabin to post a "For Sale" sign.

It includes notes of thanks for Carl and Margaret's support of fundraiser events to battle cancer, heart disease, tuberous sclerosis, birth defects, and other diseases.

But by far the largest number of notes comes from children and teens, who exhibited and then sold their goats, pigs, cows, and sheep at 4-H and FFA auctions.

Goats and Pigs and Cows and Sheep

Carl has been a fixture at livestock sales for decades, supporting youth who show and sell their animals at county fairs and local 4-H and FFA shows. Bidding at auctions to benefit others is Carl's idea of fun. He explains it this way: "Some go hunting, some go fishing, some go golfing. . . . They do all kinds of things. And I don't do any of those. But I can go sit at an auction and bid on something that's going to help . . . 4-H kids, or FFA. And I can sit there and have a ball."

But Carl doesn't attend auctions just to have fun. He brings his business savvy and bids strategically. One of his chief goals is to make sure exhibitors receive more than market value for their animals.

Lloyd explains, "He goes out to a lot of these 4-H sales and FFA sales, and buys the kids' animals. They have it set up that the butcher is there and the butcher pays, say, a dollar a pound per hog. Well, he'll make that hog bring a dollar and a quarter per pound. He'll pay the bill so the kids get good money, but then he sells it to the butcher and pays the difference. He does that with a lot of cattle and pigs and sheep."

Carl seldom trucks an animal home. What he does take with him is a feeling of satisfaction from supporting young people in their agricultural endeavors. And Lloyd points out that supporting youth at these events is a great way to put the Wenger name in front of the business's primary customers.

Carl is a fixture at the annual Lebanon County Fair, where he not only bids generously on animals, but since 2004 has given a $50 savings bond to each youth exhibiting livestock. But Carl doesn't limit his bids to local auctions. He has supported 4-H

Since 2004, Carl and Margaret have given a $50 U.S. Savings Bond to each youth who exhibits livestock at the Lebanon County Fair. The Wengers are surrounded by a sea of grateful youth in this July 2009 photo at the fairgrounds.

Giving Thanks

Carl often pays more than market value to support youth at FFA and 4-H auctions. It's harder to put a value on the many thank you notes he receives in return. Here are a few unedited excerpts:

"Thank you for your support at the Lebanon Livestock Auction. Before your offer many 4-Hers were discouraged with the prices they received. It was very generous of you to bring up the prices of the lambs."

—The Sheep Club

"Thank you so much for your support with the add-on money this year at the Putnam Co. Fair. What a surprise we had. My hog was 1st place in his class this year and I was proud of him. You made me even prouder."

—Davy

"Thanks a lot for sending me that check. I'm using it to by my next goat for the farm show."

—Jesse

"Thank You for buying my 2010 Market Hog. Your support is greatly appreciated."

—Chely

"Over the years you have supported the local 4-H & FFA in more ways than one. Words cannot express the gratitude and appreciation we have for all that you've done."

—Samantha

Thank you for coming to the 2010 Lebanon Area Fair Livestock auction! We all really appreciate your gift of a $50 savings bond. As a new member, I didn't know showing pigs could be quite so exciting and rewarding."

—Noah

"We just want to thank you for the $50.00 savings bonds. As you may know we are saving it for college."

—Hunter & Elizabeth

"Your support of programs like 4-H and FFA are such an encouragement to me and many other youth. You truly set an example for us and our community."

—Christine

"Thank you for the 50$ savings bond. I love that you gave all of use savings bonds because (well I don't know exactly how they work) but I hope its for collage because I want to be a photographer. And I think you have to go to college for that."

—Mikayla

"Thank you very much for buying my pig. Every year it is such a priviledge to raise hogs and it has taught me so many wonderful things. . . . 4-H has not only educated me about animals but through it, I have learned responsibility, respect, and leadership."

—Rachel

and FFA auctions at other locations in Pennsylvania, Maryland, Florida, and a number of other southern states.

Young people recognize Carl and appreciate his support. In addition to the many thank yous he receives—many with pictures of prize-winning steers or pigs and their proud owners—occasionally he receives notes from exhibitors inviting him to consider bidding on their animals, like one he received in 2004 from a boy named William asking Carl to consider buying his steer, Big River, at the 2004 Huntingdon County (Pa.) Fair.

One of Carl's favorite sales through the years has been the Putnam County Fair, held each March in Florida. Carl has been a supporter of the Rodeheaver Boys Ranch, near Palatka, Florida, a 790-acre operating farm and ranch that provides religious, educational, and vocational training for needy boys. The ranch has its own "Rockin' R 4-H Club," and each year about 20 boys raise and sell pigs at the county fair and get to keep the profit.

Ranch founder, Homer Rodeheaver's philosophy—"If the boys will raise the animals, the animals will raise the boys."—resonated with Carl. As a result, he bids to bring the Rodeheaver boys and other exhibitors a good return on their animals.

Carl's auction-going isn't limited to livestock sales. He is a strong supporter of a variety of benefit auctions. And just as he did when buying tractors for the business, he also plots strategy for benefit sales.

"Whenever I know they have something in multiples," explains Carl, "I try to get the first one." Friend Tom Sherk saw Carl pay $100 for a pie at an FFA benefit auction in 2009. "I talked to Carl about this pie," explains Tom, "and he said, 'Well I had to buy the first one to establish the benchmark for how the rest of these pies are going to sell.' That's how he thinks."

Because Carl gave $100 for the first pie, a few other bidders also bought at that price, before the remaining pies were put up for a second round of bidding. In the end, pies generated several hundred dollars for a good cause.

In addition to bidding generously, sometimes Carl and Margaret donate items that they purchased at previous sales to generate new support for organizations, continuing a cycle of giving. Many of their children and grandchildren also have benefitted from their auction-going when they receive beautiful quilts as gifts for weddings and other special occasions.

Talking Turkey

Another charitable effort that really took flight for Carl in his semi-retirement years was an annual turkey sale to benefit the Myerstown Lions Club. Carl has sold a lot of tractors and equipment over the years, but he may have sold even more turkeys.

When Carl joined the Lions in 1952—missing charter membership by a year—a fall fundraiser was selling dollar tickets for a chance to win one of a few dozen turkeys that the Lions Club would raffle. Give a buck, and you might win a turkey. If a Lions Club member successfully sold a book of 20 turkey tickets, he would receive a bird for his own Thanksgiving table.

Carl thought bigger than most Lions and figured selling tickets one at a time was little more than chicken—or turkey—scratch. So he changed the program to raise more money and give donors a better deal. Instead of selling individual tickets with a chance to win a bird, Carl began selling books of 20 tickets and guaranteeing a turkey for each buyer. Essentially, anyone who gave $20 to benefit the Lions Club was guaranteed a $10 turkey, with the opportunity to win additional turkeys. The Lions earned about 10 bucks per book of tickets sold.

Before long, Carl had friends and families flocking to buy turkey tickets. In the early years, he may have sold 20 or so books.

By 2007 that number had grown to 560 books, representing more than $5,000 profit for the Lions Club in a single year.

In the latter years, says Lloyd, Carl's turkey operation has become so huge that he needs to enlist the help of family members to keep records and fellow Lions to deliver birds. "He'd sit on the phone and sell them," says Lloyd, "and somebody else would do a lot of the legwork for him."

"There are people now," added daughter, Rose, early in 2009, "if they see Dad in October they'll just hand him a $20 bill. They know if they are going to come here [to Wengers] you might as well have a '20' in your pocket because you're going to get hit for it."

Fellow Lion Dr. Richard Bohn marvels at Carl's sales acumen. "He doesn't even have to say anything to the people," says Doc Bohn. "He just has a book of 20 tickets in his hand. He walks up and they whip out a $20 bill and give it to him."

The only downside of Carl's prodigious turkey sales was that, with Carl ruling the roost, the rest of the club generally sold fewer than 100 total books. "The other club members don't sell like I do," understates Carl.

Then again, with Carl gobbling up sales, it's hard to get down on his colleagues. It's a little like Grandson Joshua Wenger said: "There was no one left to sell to."

Naming Rights

While benevolent bids at auctions and hawking turkeys are ways of giving that especially suit Carl's style, he supports many organizations in more traditional ways. When Evangelical Seminary in Myerstown sought to expand what the new master's program in Marriage and Family Therapy could offer, they went to Carl and Margaret, who had supported the seminary in the past—and who had been successfully married for more than 50 years.

Then seminary President Dr. Kirby Keller, who served alongside Carl in the local Rotary Club, laid out the seminary's vision during a winter visit to Carl and Margaret's Florida home. The goal was to renovate facilities for a new counseling center so that the seminary could simultaneously train new therapists and assist struggling families, couples, and individuals in the community. It would require $100,000 for the vision to become reality.

Between Carl and Margaret's generous lead donation to the campaign, given over five years, and additional funding from the Wenger Foundation, in May 2006 the seminary opened the doors to The Wenger Family Counseling Center (renamed The Wenger Marriage & Family Center in 2011) at the seminary campus in Myerstown.

The center now serves as a training facility for advanced graduate students in the seminary's Marriage and Family Therapy master's program, with qualified intern therapists providing counseling under the supervision of licensed marriage and family therapists. According to the Marriage & Family Therapy Program Director, Joy E. Corby, Ph.D., since the center's beginning, intern therapists have served over 230 "units," with the number served growing gradually each year. (A unit may be an individual, couple, or family.)

"The students get the training they need," says Carl with satisfaction, "and the community has the availability of affordable counseling."

Responsive to First Responders

Providing funding for a counseling center was something new for Carl and Margaret, but their commitment to disaster relief and those who assist others in times of need continued. In addition to their regular support of Church of the

Carl and Margaret twice donated equipment to the Florida Baptist Convention. They gave a bucket truck in 2005 to assist with Hurricane Katrina clean up and a forklift in 2009 to pack supplies for Haiti earthquake relief. Pictured with both pieces in this 2009 photo are (from left) Baptist Disaster staff Terry Ryan, Carl, Margaret, and Lloyd Wenger. Photo by Kitty Wenger.

Brethren disaster relief through the annual Brethren Disaster Relief Auction, in 2005 Carl and Margaret branched out to help Baptist relief efforts. They were recognized in the *Lebanon Daily News* for donating a 1997 GMC bucket truck—bedecked with Wengers of Myerstown insignia—to the Disaster Relief Team of the Florida Baptist Convention in Orange Park, Florida, to help with Gulf Coast cleanup following the devastation of Hurricane Katrina. In February 2009, Carl and Margaret donated a forklift to the Baptists to assist with loading supplies for earthquake relief in Haiti.

When floodwaters generated by Hurricane Irene and Tropical Storm Lee inundated Central Pennsylvania in September 2011, Carl again responded—this time to recognize first responders who came to the aid of others. With Carl spearheading the effort and daughter Rose handling details, the Wenger Foundation sponsored a Lebanon County First Responders Appreciation Banquet on December 13.

The foundation actually had sponsored a similar event in 1997 at the Lantern Lodge in Myerstown for Eastern Lebanon County first responders from Richland, Myerstown, Newmanstown, and Schaefferstown fire companies. As it turned out, the venue was too small, and some had to be turned away.

Having learned from that experience, the Foundation booked the spacious Lebanon Expo Center for the 2011 event and invited first responders from all of Lebanon County. More than 400 people enjoyed a meal and live entertainment as an expression of the community's thanks for their sacrifices. The event was sponsored by the Wengers and other area businesses.

Speaking to a Fox 43 News reporter covering the banquet, Rose explained why the Wengers felt it was important to recognize first responders: "They're called away from their homes at night," she said. "They're going into dangerous situations. They're leaving the comfort of their homes and families, and I just think it's important to say thank you."

Lebanon County firefighter and Chairman of the Lebanon County Firefighters Association Building Committee Chuck Killian (left) and City of Lebanon Fire Commissioner Duane Trautman were among the many first responders honored at a December 2011 dinner sponsored by the Wenger Foundation. Photo by Rick Harpel.

A Philosophy of Giving

At a special event in April 2006, members of the Myerstown community felt it was time to say thank you to Carl, as well, for all he had done to benefit others. At a banquet, held at the Lantern Lodge Ballroom on May 19, 2006, the Lebanon Valley Sertoma Club honored Carl with its Service to Mankind Award and the accompanying J. Robert Ladd Community Service Award.

The tribute in the printed program specifically mentioned Carl's longtime support of the Brethren Disaster Relief Auction and Lebanon Valley Brethren Home; his role in launching the Wenger Counseling Center at Evangelical Seminary; his prodigious turkey sales and nearly 60 years of service through the local Lions Club; his life-long commitment to FFA; and the ongoing work of the Wenger Foundation.

The event included a roast of Carl, with friends Glen "Bud" Mitstifer, Dr. Richard Bohn, John Kline, and Sam Hayes serving up stories to show appreciation for—and to embarrass—the guest of honor.

The Sertoma award provided Carl with an opportunity to discuss how the man known for the big hat had become better known for his big heart. Carl confessed to a *Lebanon Daily News* reporter that he wasn't always a generous giver. "I was brought up as very conservative," he explained, "but not as benevolent."

While his parents frequently helped people they encountered through the store in Rexmont, they didn't serve as philanthropic role models for Carl. "My parents helped a lot of people," he says, "but I didn't necessarily get my training from them."

Instead, Carl credits mentor Carlos Leffler—another Church of the Brethren member and founder of what became Leffler Energy—with teaching and inspiring him to become a generous giver.

"I was friends with Carlos Leffler," Carl explains, "and he was always doing something and supporting something financially. He would call me and say, 'I need $500 for this at the library' or 'Send me $500 for this or that.' I kept watching him."

What Carl saw in Leffler was a man who gave frequently, generously, and openly, with his name prominently displayed on facilities like Elizabethtown College's Leffler Chapel and Performance Center. And Carl liked what he saw and has tried to emulate it by also giving in ways that other people can see.

Not everyone appreciates Carl's penchant for giving in ways that garner recognition, but he has a clear idea of what he is trying to accomplish.

Alluding to Jesus' teaching in Matthew 6 that giving to the needy should be done in secret, Carl explains, "We were brought up Brethren, where the right hand isn't supposed to know what the left hand is doing and all this. I totally disagree with that."

Carl believes in giving openly so others are inspired to follow his example. Photo by Ron Yedinak.

Carl agrees with Jesus that it is wrong to give to win the applause of other people. "If you give to get recognition," he concedes, "that's wrong." But, he adds, "If you do it for an example, that's good."

Carl admits that it's a fine line, but insists that he would not give as much as he does today, were it not for the examples of others who showed him the way. He hopes that his example of generous giving will,

You Win Some, You Lose Some

Carl loves to tell stories of people he encountered and helped during his travels. He relates two stories that illustrate the risks and rewards of playing the Good Samaritan. First the rewards.

One January evening in Florida in 1991, Carl and Margaret were traveling home from a church service, when they spotted an African American family with van trouble on the opposite side of busy Interstate 4. Carl exited the eastbound highway and returned to the family in distress on the westbound side.

"I figured we were in church and we were on the way home," Carl explains. "If he's in trouble and we don't stop to help, it was no use we went to church because we didn't learn much."

The family was returning home from North Carolina, passing through the area, and had nothing more than a gas card with them. The father, a man named Alvin, explained to Carl that he didn't know what to do. Carl did. He located a policeman to help get the vehicle safely off the road, he put the family up for the night in a local hotel, and he called his own mechanic and told him to tow and fix the disabled van.

Carl assured his mechanic that he would pay the bill if the traveler was unable to. The incredulous mechanic scratched his head and did as he was told, sure that Carl would never be repaid. What Carl didn't realize was that the family not only didn't have money with them, they didn't have money at home either.

Carl paid the $160 auto repair bill and the hotel bill, and a short time later received a thank you note from the family. Four months later he received a longer letter from Alvin, introducing his family and situation, and again expressing thanks. Alvin enclosed a check for $110, all the family could afford at the time.

Carl filed the letter and a copy of the check away with the auto repair bill and was pleased that he had done a good turn. He thought that was the end of it, until a decade later his phone rang. It was Alvin.

"He said, 'You probably don't remember me,'" says Carl. But for some reason Carl instantly recognized the voice. "He told me how his children had graduated and how good he was getting along and all these things. And he thanked me one more time for helping him 10 years before."

Carl still has his "Alvin file" and marvels that a man would remember an act of kindness for a decade and take the time to call and say thank you.

Another episode with a traveler didn't have such a happy ending.

On a flight home from Columbus, Ohio, Carl, Margaret, and Rose struck up a conversation with a young man in the military, who was traveling home for the weekend. When their flight arrived late, it appeared the young man would be stranded in Pittsburgh.

Because the soldier was too young to rent his own car, Carl rented a car for him and sent him on his way. The young man assured Carl that he could pay Carl back. "He gave me a good snow job," Carl recounts.

About a week later Carl began to have an uneasy feeling and called the rental company. The car had not been returned. Now Carl had a problem. They only could remember the young man's last name and the general area where he was going. After multiple phone calls, they finally located the soldier's adoptive father, who did not have good news for them.

The young man had got into a fight, wrecked the car, and landed in jail. Jaded by the boy's long history of trouble, the father refused any help to the Wengers. "You got yourself into this mess," he said. "You get yourself out. That boy's been nothing but trouble ever since we had him."

Carl made his confession to the rental car company and paid a hefty bill. But he didn't stop taking chances.

"The thing you always have to remember when you get one like that," he explains, "is that you daren't hold that against the next opportunity you get, or you won't do it. And then you'll miss the right one, the one you ought to be doing."

in turn, inspire others to join him in meeting the needs of their community and world. If someone sees his name on the back of a fundraiser event t-shirt, Carl hopes that will inspire them to give to get their name on the shirt the next time.

"I think if people can see you do it," he concludes, "but not do it boastfully, you can teach people how to do it. Sometimes showing them is the best way."

And there's no question Carl does have a penchant for giving in ways that inspire others to join him, whether by establishing the price for the first pie at a benefit auction, selling turkeys to support the Lions Club, or on a larger scale when he invites other business leaders and individuals to join him in supporting worthy causes through the annual Praise Dinner.

Giving has become such a priority for Carl that for the past decade or more he has sometimes given money that he doesn't even have—at least not freely available. "I never had money," Carl explains. "I always invested it or did something else with it." To facilitate giving, Carl established a line of credit with a local bank. "I give the money away off the credit line," he explains, "and then I go back and replace it." Carl believes that this approach enables him to be more nimble in responding to needs. If he is attracted to a cause, he gives immediately and worries later about which of his assets he will pull it from. Otherwise, he says, he would never have money free to give away.

As he contemplates his legacy, Carl hopes that, more than anything else, others will remember him for the ways in which he helped people.

A Dream Demolished

While Carl is at his best when helping others, in 2008 he encountered two situations, where he needed to rely on help from others. He received the help he needed to overcome a life-

threatening illness, but was not able to muster enough support
to save a building that he considered a precious part of his and
his community's heritage.

As Carl prepared to travel to Florida for eye surgery in
June 2008 he became aware that the Cornwall-Lebanon School
Board was about to demolish the historic Cornwall redbrick
schoolhouse. Built in 1901 on an acre of land purchased from
Cornwall Furnace owner Robert Coleman, the neo-classical
revival-style building initially was a high school for grades 9
through 11.

When a new limestone school, which today is Cornwall
Elementary School, opened across the street in 1928—connect-
ed to the old school by an underground walkway passing under
Route 419—the redbrick school was used chiefly as a vocational
building for shop and ag classes, art, and home economics. The
schoolhouse became a storage and maintenance facility when
Cedar Crest Middle School opened its doors in 1972.

Many people in the community appreciated the building's
history and architecture, but Carl's connections were more personal. His father had been in the first graduating class at the
redbrick school, and his mother also had graduated from there.
Margaret attended classes in the brick building, and Carl, himself, had begun his FFA career there. He held fond memories of
restoring a manure spreader in the school's daylight basement.

Carl had known the fate of the old school was under discussion, but he believed there was enough community support to
safeguard its future. The Lebanon Valley Conservancy, Cornwall
Borough, and the Cornwall Historical Alliance, formed in 2005,
had been collaborating to save the schoolhouse.

But after three-and-a-half years of debate, on June 16, 2008,
the School Board rejected a final pitch from the Conservancy to
lease the building while it continued to pursue funding for preservation. Tired of the protracted discussions, the board voted 5-4
to raze the building and awarded a $59,500 demolition contract to

Going. Going. Gone. Despite Carl's late bid to save it, the Cornwall Redbrick school-house was demolished in summer 2008. Photos by Melissa Long. Used by permission.

Musser's Excavating of Lititz. The building's death sentence was to be carried out prior to the start of school on August 25.

At a disadvantage because he was in Florida recovering from surgery, Carl nevertheless threw himself into obtaining a stay of execution for the beloved schoolhouse. He initially contacted Superintendent Tom Sherk, who turned out to be a first cousin, once removed, of Carl's. Tom had great respect for Carl's parents, who had once done his family a good turn.

The superintendent agreed to e-mail board members to let them know of Carl's interest in saving the building. Though Carl felt Tom was sympathetic, ultimately it was a board decision. So Carl obtained the phone numbers of all nine board members and launched an old school lobbying effort, employing his considerable powers of persuasion to convince individual board members to reverse their decision. Some refused to talk, and others were unsympathetic, but Carl offered those who would listen 100,000 reasons to reconsider. Privately, he entertained visions of restoring the school to house a Christian youth ministry or some other enterprise that would be of benefit to the community.

Carl's $100,000 offer to buy the building was enough to motivate several board members to convince board president Gary Watts to call a special meeting on Friday, July 11, to take another look at the board's decision. Still marooned in Florida, Carl was unable to attend, but was confident he had the five votes he needed to save the school. But he was wrong.

According to *Lebanon Daily News* and *Harrisburg Patriot News* coverage of the meeting, because the board already had signed a contract with a demolition company, it felt it needed $100,000 just to serve as an indemnity bond to protect itself from legal action that could ensue from terminating the contract—this even though the contract was for less than $60,000. In addition, the $100,000 that Carl already had offered was to purchase the building—which the district did not want to sell because they wanted to keep the land for parking or other potential uses. At the meeting, it was unclear to the board how Carl's offer would apply toward the Conservancy plan to lease and restore the building.

At one point during the rancorous meeting, Conservancy attorney Wiley Parker placed a call to Carl in Florida to ask if he would extend a $100,000 line of credit to the district to tap in case of legal action. After the 10-minute conversation, Wiley returned and reported that Carl was prepared to issue an immediate letter of credit for $20,000, apparently in addition to the original $100,000 purchase offer.

But weary of more than three years of discussion, already committed to a contract for the building's imminent demolition, and uncertain of how much Carl would give for purposes other than outright purchase of the building, the board voted 7-1 against a motion to delay razing of the school. The battle was lost. Demolition began a short time later and was completed in August 2008. Carl stopped over to watch the process one day and came away with a truckload of bricks as mementos.

Time may cause him to re-evaluate, but nearly a year after the schoolhouse came down Carl ranked its destruction as the second greatest loss of his life, surpassed only by the death of his granddaughter.

Illness Overcome

A few months after the school came down, Carl faced another challenge with much more at stake than a building. Scheduled for knee replacement surgery on October 14, 2008, Carl wasn't feeling well. He headed to Good Samaritan Hospital in Lebanon a day early to get checked out. Little did he know when he entered the hospital that he would face potentially life-threatening surgery and wouldn't return home for nearly a month.

Testing at both Good Samaritan and the Penn State Hershey Medical Center revealed a tennis ball-size tumor in Carl's abdomen and a potentially life-threatening aneurism. Carl was scheduled for surgery several days later, on Monday, October 20. Surgeons told Carl it would be wise for him to make sure he had his affairs in order before entering the operating room for an expected seven hours or more of surgery to remove the tumor and repair the aneurism.

Carl called his family together and talked a little about his funeral. The service was to be at the Lebanon Expo Center, where Carl had spent many hours of his life at auctions, agricultural events, and Wenger Foundation Praise Dinners. Burial was to be across Evergreen Road in the cemetery at the Midway Church of the Brethren, where Carl had begun his walk with Jesus. He even instructed how he wished to be transported from the memorial service to the cemetery—on a farm wagon pulled by his beloved 1952 Farmall H, the first new tractor he ever sold.

Facing serious surgery in 2008, Carl made funeral plans. Among his stated wishes was that his casket be loaded on a farm wagon and pulled to the Midway cemetery by his beloved 1952 Farmall H tractor. The tractor was the first new tractor that he ever sold. Many years later he bought it back and had it restored to pristine condition. Fortunately, Carl's surgery restored him, as well, and the tractor didn't need to be pressed into service.

But Carl wasn't ready for his final tractor ride just yet. In addition to setting things in order, he also had friends and family put out a call for prayer.

"I can't share prayer like a lot of my friends," Carl confesses, "but I have great faith in prayer. And at that point we put the word out in as many ways as possible to my friends around the country. If ever I needed help I would need it that Monday.

"I went to the doctors and told them that they would be working under more prayer that Monday morning than they had ever worked under before," he continues. "I just assured them that was the way it was going to be. I am sure it was that way."

Bathed in prayer, Carl was at peace as he entered surgery. The surgery went more quickly than expected and was successful. "They were astonished at how well it worked for them," says Carl, referring to the doctors. "Nobody said that prayer was the answer to all of that; but we all felt it. It was a great experience."

Carl was so appreciative of the care he had received at Good Samaritan that he took the time to pen a letter to the editor of the *Lebanon Daily News*, thanking everyone from surgeons Bryan Pilkington and Benson Harvey to the cleaning and dietary staff for the exceptional care he had received.

He concluded his letter: "I know that there is much wrong with today's world, but after my ordeal, I am much more in-clined to view the abundant amount of positive that is part of our lives each day."

Carl also came home from the hospital determined to use wisely the extra time that he had been given. "I value this time very highly," he explained. "It is bonus time and I want to do everything I can to the highest degree of success."

Living Legacy

Following his surgery, Carl backed off from daily in-volvement in the business. Margaret points to his 2008 hos-pitalization as the time when he finally retired; although he continues to take on projects for the business with his chil-dren's permission and buy salvage tractors *without* their per-mission.

He maintains a corner office in the construction building along Route 501, but he doesn't visit it often. He is less involved in the day-to-day aspects of the business now than at any time in his life. He no longer carries a key to the building, but his legacy lives on at Wengers of Myerstown.

Son Glenn is grateful for the "solid foundation that we could build on" that his father bequeathed to his children. Carl's willingness to take risks, his superior sales acumen, and commitment to careful record keeping all continue to find expression in the business his children now operate.

Systems that Carl put in place four decades ago, says Glenn, continue to serve the company well today. "Sure we've taken them from paper to computer," he explains, "but it's the same system." He credits his dad with always understanding the importance of solid monthly financial statements. "You knew where you were at, whether it was good or bad," he says. "That carries forward today. And I give Dad a tremendous amount of credit for that."

Glenn wonders what he and his siblings would have become, were Carl not the entrepreneur that he was. Would any of them have had the skills and courage to build a business from the ground up like their father did? Indeed, it is hard to imagine the Wenger family without the Wenger family of companies.

Carl's legacy includes much more than a business. He and Margaret are now parents of seven, grandparents of 13, and have been blessed with 10 great-grandchildren. Pictured here in the early 1990s are their 14 grandchildren.

His Creed

Carl is a plain-spoken, practical man, not given to flowery language and high-sounding talk. But he does have one treatise that he likes to share. Written by statesman Dean Alfange, "My Creed," or "An American Creed," appeared in *Reader's Digest* during the 1950s and has become a favorite in some conservative circles. The statement's emphasis on opportunity and self-reliance resonates with Carl:

> *I do not choose to be a common man. It is my right to be uncommon—if I can. I seek opportunity—not security. I do not wish to be a kept citizen, humbled and dulled by having the state look after me. I want to take the calculated risk; to dream and to build, to fail and to succeed. I refuse to barter incentive for a dole. I prefer the challenges of life to the guaranteed existence; the thrill of fulfillment to the stale calm of utopia. I will not trade freedom for beneficence nor my dignity for a handout. I will never cower before any master nor bend to any threat. It is my heritage to stand erect, proud and unafraid; to think and act for myself, enjoy the benefit of my creations, and to face the world boldly and say, this I have done. All this is what it means to be an American.*

Carl can take great satisfaction in the business and business sense that he passed on to his progeny.

The View from White Park Way

Carl came away from his serious illness with a renewed resolve to make sure Margaret was cared for if something were to happen to him. As he got his affairs in order prior to surgery, Carl spoke to some of his children about caring for their mother and providing a more suitable house for her. He worried about Margaret rattling around in a large farmhouse, burdened with two stories of cleaning and cares.

Carl and Margaret have a comfortable retirement home that sits on a rise overlooking the farm where they built a family and a business. Pictured are the house and a panoramic view from the front yard.

When he came through surgery successfully, at the age of 78 Carl took the task of building a house upon himself, and he and Margaret began making plans for their retirement home. They chose a contractor to build a comfortable, but stately, one-story home on a rise on the edge of the Wenger farm, just a stone's throw from the farmhouse where they set up housekeeping and raised their family. Along Park Street is an unofficial street sign, denoting their driveway as "White Park Way."

Located at the corner of Park and Race Streets, their new home afforded Carl and Margaret the opportunity to look back over a lifetime of memories and achievements. From their front porch, they could gaze upon the clear waters of the Tulpehocken Creek, winding its way through the meadow that

Carl hiked through after school during his early teen years when his teacher dropped him off along Route 501. It was the same meadow where Carl and Margaret took Sunday afternoon walks during their dating days to make sure the electric fence wasn't compromised by weeds. It was the meadow where their dairy herd once grazed, and where Carl took a hoe to more than one thistle during his latter years. Today Wenger Farms' White Park Cattle chew on the pasture's lush grasses and continue Carl's legacy of farming.

Just a quarter mile to the south, Carl and Margaret can see their historic 1799 farmhouse, where they set up housekeeping; raised seven children; and began a business, meeting customers at the kitchen table. Later, grandchildren splashed in the backyard pool there on warm summer days. Some of those same grandchildren today are employed in the family business that Carl began, carrying on his legacy.

In addition to the view of the farmhouse where they raised their own children, Carl and Margaret can see the homes where all three of their daughters have raised theirs. Their four sons each live with their families within a few miles of home, as well, reminding Carl that he and Margaret have built more than a business.

Across Race Street from the old farmhouse there's the modest three-bay garage, with wooden sliding doors, where Carl tore apart his first "used and abused" tractors and later parked his first new Cadillac. It's a reminder of his business' humble beginnings and what can be accomplished through determination and hard work.

Along Park Street they can see land that once served as truck patches, where Carl first raised award-winning crops of tomatoes for the Campbell's Soup Company and where migrant workers later helped Carl and Margaret harvest acres of the juicy fruits. In fact, their house now stands in what once was a patch of tomatoes.

Carl views the time since his surgery in 2008 as a gift to be used to benefit others. He and Margaret enjoy time together in this December 2009 photo.

Looking to the south, there's the first shop that Carl built in 1964 at 251 South Race Street to house his growing Wenger's Farm Machinery, Inc. He can picture his aging father sitting at the entrance of that building, drinking a Coke and greeting customers, and remember the many ways his parents helped shape him into the person and businessman that he became. Today the machine shop operates in that building, where son-in-law "Wally" Walmer oversees a growing component of the Wenger family of companies.

Beyond the buildings are acres and acres of fields, where Carl first farmed and then displayed farm equipment for his customers. As he scans the grounds where his business once was centered, his mind is flooded with images of deals closed, auctions held, customers served, crises overcome, relationships built. With the core of the business relocated to new facilities a few miles away, today many of those fields that once were covered with used tractors and implements have returned to farming. But Carl remembers not only the crops, but the business that he grew in those fields on the southwest edge of Myerstown.

On the eve of his 80th birthday, it would be understandable if Carl were to spend all of his time sitting on the porch of his retirement home, gazing back upon a lifetime of memories and achievements. But he doesn't have time.

From his new home, Carl also can see other things. Behind the house is the community of Myerstown, which he has served for more than six decades. And beyond that a world of need. He can see fire companies and service clubs responding to the needs of his community; the local, regional, and worldwide ministries of his church; organizations in Myerstown and beyond

Carl isn't the only one in the family with a big hat. Their children surprised Carl and Margaret by staging a western theme photo shoot on the farm in summer 2011 and presenting the photos to Carl and Margaret as a Christmas gift. Standing are Rose and Larry. Seated from left are Glenn, Nancy, Lloyd, Carol, and Davey. Photo by Kitty Wenger.

serving children and youth; retirement communities caring for the elderly; colleges and seminaries raising up leaders for the future; missionaries meeting human needs and telling the story of Jesus; public figures and national radio ministries seeking to shape the country and the culture.

Carl can see a world where disasters strike, families struggle, and basic needs go unmet. And he can see that he has a role to play in meeting the needs of others as he shares a lifetime of blessings. Once known as the imposing figure with the big hat at farm auctions throughout the country, today Carl is recognized as the kindly man with the big heart at fundraisers, auctions, and community events. At age 80, he's still looking for opportunities to do more, give more, serve more. Somewhere along the way the man with the big hat became the man with the big heart.

With a lifetime of achievement behind him, Carl still is looking for opportunities ahead of him and will be as long as he has health and strength. You can hang your hat on that.

Memory Pages

Friends and family members were asked to share memories for this project. We are grateful for the following stories, insights, and tributes, most of which were submitted in the first half of 2009. Sadly, since then three contributors—Robert Bailey, Rodger Bowman, and Earl Forney—have passed away.

Pat Adams, Friend, Myerstown, Pa.

I have known Carl for many years. His name and business are Myerstown! I first met him in the banking field at the local Farmer's Trust Bank. We have shared a friendship ever since. Through banking and community interaction, walking past his home and being friends with his children, we have continued to enjoy each other's stories. Most recently I had the privilege of attending a Wenger Praise Dinner. Carl had invited me on numerous occasions, but we were not able to do so until this year (2009). It was an experience! I hope to enjoy the dinner from this year forward.

Harry H. Bachman, Auctioneer, Friend, Distant Relative, Annville, Pa.

I have known Carl a long time by him attending auctions, as well as doing the 4-H livestock auctions, where Carl and Margaret have been longtime supporters. The last several years they have provided savings bonds to the members of the Lebanon County 4-H Livestock Club. Not only does he provide these bonds, but he also makes sure that all of the exhibitors receive a fair value for their market animals.

Carl likes to tell the story that when people see him and myself with our cowboy hats they think that I am Carl and vice versa. I was in Florida attending a large auction, and the owner of the company insisted that I was Carl Wenger, until one of the auctioneers finally convinced him that I wasn't him. Carl and myself are distant relatives, so perhaps that is what makes us have some of the same features.

Several years ago I discussed an issue with Carl in regards to the sudden death of good friend Bryan Crouse. Bryan had two children in 4-H, so I discussed with Carl how we could raise money to support these two boys with their projects. We decided to sell $50 shares and then get together before the Friday evening auction to see how well we did. We had collected over $12,000, which was used to support these two boys' projects.

Carl is a true gentleman and is always looking for new ways to lend support to a lot of worthwhile projects. When he sees me at the Brethren Disaster Relief Auction, he reminds me that it is "turkey time." His ability to contribute to many projects is definitely a talent that not many people possess. We can truly say that knowing him has been an inspiration to us, and we certainly value our friendship. Along with his lovely wife, Margaret, they have raised a model family, who has also contributed much to everyone that they meet and associate with.

Robert A. Bailey, Friend, Business Associate, Richland, Pa.

I used to own the Kumm Esse Diner in Myerstown, and I got to know Carl well because enjoying food was one of his favorite pastimes. We also visited Carl and Margaret a couple times in Florida. When we talked about going out for dinner, we all agreed to leave at 5:30 p.m. When the time to go arrived, Carl would say, "I just have one phone call to make," and that he would need about five minutes. Approximately 45 minutes later, we were on our way, when Carl casually mentioned that he wanted to stop and talk to a business friend along the way. After another 45 minutes, we finally drove off to the restaurant. Luckily, we still were hungry and did not lose our appetites!

Another time, when the guys were traveling to a NASCAR race at Talladega, in Alabama, we stopped at a restaurant serving a buffet dinner. I remember getting some food for Carl, as did one of our other friends. By that time Carl had finished two platters, and we were just getting started. I mentioned to John Smith that we seemed to be doing this the wrong way!

A lot of our good times revolved around food, but Carl's best times are all community oriented, relating to the good he does for different organizations and people. We could certainly use more of his type in our community.

Carol Behney, Former Employee, Friend, Myerstown, Pa.

I remember walking into the old Wenger office, on Race Street, for an interview with Carl in October 1969. I was scared, nervous, and had no previous office experience, but was good in math and willing to learn. Carl stated that he would teach me all my duties as we went along and hired me. So began my career with the Wenger family. My stay of employment was to last 32 years, until I finally retired in early 2001. As an employer, Carl was always understanding if I needed to be home with sick kids or family matters. He was always concerned and caring.

I, along with my husband, Bill, became close to Carl, Margaret, and their family. Outside the workplace we spent many fun weekends car racing with son Davey. Bill even stayed with Carl in Florida for a Daytona race adventure.

Carl was always generous to both of us, and we remain friends today.

Carol Blecker, Friend, Lebanon, Pa.

I had known of Carl and Margaret Wenger for years through their children, who attended the same high school as my husband. Unfortunately, what brought us together as friends was tragedy. During the summer of 1994 Carl and Margaret tragically lost a granddaughter, and in January 1995 I lost my husband to a tragic accident. We became friends because we had this in common.

Carl and Margaret invited me to attend various events with them, and I got to know his family better. I complimented him on having a wonderful family, and he credited Margaret for doing a fine job raising them while he worked. He has been a very caring, giving person to his church and community. Often unknown to others, he shares the gifts God has blessed him with.

Paul H. Boll, Former Executive Director, Lebanon Valley Brethren Home, Palmyra, Pa.

It was the summer of 1979. We had just moved to Palmyra. My wife, Carol's, parents were visiting with us for the week. We were showing them around the area, and her father asked if we could look up Rev. L. John Weaver, pastor of the Midway Church of the Brethren. He was a classmate of Carol's father in the Johnstown area. We had directions, but were uncertain which house was the parsonage. We stopped in front of the house and were attempting to make certain it was the correct place when a pick up truck stopped and the driver asked if we needed help. It was Carl Wenger, the man with the big hat. Carl had not only a big hat, but a big heart. He shared with us about the church and the community. There was no question as to his knowledge and his involvement. It was the beginning of a lasting friendship.

It was a few weeks later that Mr. Bob DiMatteo, Mr. Carlos Leffler, and I met at a restaurant near Myerstown to have lunch with Carl in anticipation of his willingness to become a board member at the Lebanon Valley Brethren Home. I recall Carl's immediate concern: He said that he did not have a lot of experience in health care, but would be willing to do whatever he could for the home. He became a board member and ended up having more experience in health care than he thought. But more important was his experience in the area of development.

Needless to say, there's a great need to assist persons in retirement facilities who are no longer able to pay for their care. Carl was very involved in the establishment of our Good Samaritan Fund. Each year we have two special events to support the fund: a Chicken BBQ and Auction and the Good Samaritan Fund Benefit Dinner. Carl has been very involved with both, but especially with the auction. Each year as the auction was about to begin I was so thrilled to see the man with the big hat seated in the audience.

Not only Carl, but also his family has served the home. His wife, Margaret, daughter-in-law Kitty and son Glenn have assisted with the BBQ and auction. Kitty was President of the Auxiliary and co-chaired the BBQ committee with Glenn, who has been securing the auctioneers and personally served as one of them for many years. They have been and continue to be God's sent to provide for others.

The Lebanon Valley Brethren Home continues to be blessed by the Wenger family because of the leadership and encouragement of Carl. And that's not only true of the home, but also of the church and community. Carl truly is the man with the big hat but, more importantly, he's the man with the big heart. He's not only ready to give of himself and all he has, but is able to help others realize the importance of giving. Giving is such an important part of his life. We are thrilled to share in telling Carl's life story. May the Good Lord continue to bless and use him as a blessing to others.

David C. Bond, Friend, Business Associate, Ringoes, N.J.

My relationship with Carl Wenger began when I was 11 or 12 years old. My father and I would travel 120 miles to Elizabethtown, Pennsylvania, to attend G.K. Wagner's monthly machinery auction. Carl was starting his business, buying and selling farm equipment, and was a regular buyer at that auction.

It was at one of these sales that Carl talked my father into coming to his farm to look at a four-row corn planter. When we finally got there, I spotted a trailer load of four brand new Farmall 400 tractors sitting next to the barn. I remember the trailer was pulled by a 1952 or 1953 GMC. Carl said that they had just come in from Ohio. I can still remember thinking to myself that buying and selling farm equipment is what I wanted to do when I grow up.

My dad and Carl's dad would talk about Carl jumping into the used equipment business. His dad chuckled as he pointed to the sign hanging at the corner of the driveway that read, "New, Used & Abused Tractors & Farm Machinery."

As the years passed, I finished high school and did some business with Carl. One day he was traveling in our area and stopped in to ask if I was going to a nearby auction that Saturday. I said that I was, so we drove to the site and looked at the equipment. Carl left me some prices, and I ended up buying him a John Deere A and a couple other items. For the next couple years I bought a few tractors and a number of Allis Chalmers round balers for Carl. He treated me well, never arguing about price or quality. He just wrote me a check and said, "Thank you!"

In 1959 I attended Rutgers University for a short time. I must say that I learned more riding with Carl for a couple hours than I did during my time at Rutgers. He said, "Keep one thing in mind. Buy cheap, sell high, be honest and fair, and don't get too greedy."

In 1968, my neighbor, Roger Everitt, and I began buying and selling farm equipment and soon formed a partnership, D and R Equipment, Inc. Roger and I did a lot of business with Carl. We would go to Myerstown in late afternoon or early evening and usually would buy a load or two of tractors. I can remember Carl coming out of the dairy barn to sell us equipment. Margaret would finish the milking!

Carl was always sure that if a customer wanted something, he could find it for him. Carl was a great salesman. I can remember saying that I really liked his 1972 dark green Cadillac Coupe de Ville. Forty-five minutes later I was headed back to New Jersey in my 1972 dark green, Cadillac Coupe de Ville!

I could go on for hours about my relationship with Carl. I want to point out the fact that he always had time to share a story with his friends and took time for his family and church. I am proud to be a friend of Carl Wenger.

David R. Bowman, Cousin, Palmyra, Pa.

When Carl and I were young (before TV and other distractions), we knew our uncles and aunts and cousins, and visits were frequent. It was always a joy to see John Wenger's car come up our farm lane in South Annville Township, but this one particular time Aunt Bertha was carrying a little bundle, who they had named Carl. I didn't know how he would fit into the relation because his first year he didn't even speak to us.

He grew up to be a nice young man, and pretty soon Margaret used up most of his time. It soon became apparent that Carl and Margaret spent much of their time finding new ways to do more good things for more people. Thankfully, we were on that list too. I have attended more than one honorary dinner for Carl, and I finally summed it up by saying, "Cousin Carl, it serves you right."

J. Clyde Bowman, Friend, Dayton, Va.

I'm writing these lines regarding times with Carl Wenger, which go back to school days. He was a respected man in the community and all surrounding areas, plus known in all areas of the county as Wenger's Farm Machinery. I worked for Carl when the business was on Race Street. When asked what makes Carl "tick," he had a yearning to buy and sell farm machinery in high school years. Now I have only good to say for Carl Wenger. Carl, now that both of us have met the "three score and ten," beyond that are bonus years for us.

Mr. and Mrs. Rodger Bowman, Friend and "Cousin," Cleona, Pa.

Carl's father, John, and my grandmother Frany, were brother and sister. Carl is a cousin to my late father, Lloyd Bowman. As a kid, I remember Carl and other family members throwing horse shoes at family get-togethers. Carl is a good guy and kept his family together with the business park in Myerstown. When we see Carl and wife and children at car shows and the motorcycle store, we call each other "cousin" and chat a bit. I am proud to be part of the Wenger family.

Paul Boyer, Friend, Quentin, Pa.

Help me draw a mental picture
    of how a good man should be.
This man would have to love the Lord
    and love his family.

He'd face each task that came his way
    and give it his very best.
No matter how hard that task might be,
    he would manage to pass the test.

Now you have to add some courage
    to help him overcome
The many hills he will have to climb
    before his life is done.

Fill in around him lots of friends,
    there would be many indeed.
And the kind of a man we're drawing here
    would always help those in need.

Don't forget to draw in a church
    where this man would faithfully serve.
Here he gains the strength to travel life's road,
    overcoming the bumps and the curves.

Now we're almost finished,
    but one thing we need to make our picture complete.
The Lord overlooking the life that we've drawn
    with a smile and a look discrete.

As he nods his approval to everything here,
    the kind of picture we see

Is a husband, a father, a grandpa, a friend.
How a good man's life should be.

Now we look at the picture, look real hard
    to find out who it could be.
The image comes clearer and clearer,
    Carl Wenger is the man we see.

Barbara Brooks, RN, Coumadin Nurse, DeLand, Fla.

I have known Mr. Wenger since January 2004. I think he has
a great attitude about life. He always has a kind word to say, no
matter what he personally is going through in his life. He can
brighten up your day with his smile. He also brings us the yum-
miest pretzels each year! As long as he keeps smiling, this world
is bound to be a better place. His smile is very contagious.

Rich Brandt, Realtor, Longtime Friend, Newmanstown, Pa.

I have known Carl Wenger for six decades.
    In the '50s: I first met Carl when I purchased a Farmall
Cub tractor and Carl financed it. I fell on hard times, and Carl
worked with me on paying him back.
    In the '60s: Carl, Carlos Leffler, Bill Schaeffer, and I togeth-
er attended a Dale Carnegie course on "How to Win Friends
and Influence People." We all recalled on that course several
times, as time passed in our lives.
    In the '70s (and thereafter): Carl always supported the 4-H
and FFA kids. When there was an auction for their animals, Carl
would come to me and say, "Rich, I need you to bid me up on
the sale." He wanted to make sure the kids would get a fair price
for their stock. All the high bidders were willing to spend a lot

on a champion animal because they received publicity, but Carl spent a lot of money on the total sale so many kids would have a decent price for their animal. Carl never got the recognition he deserved for this.

In the '80s: In 1982 the farm economy, along with the business economy, was at the bottom of the barrel. No one had money to promote and support the Lebanon Farm Show Livestock Auction. Normally the Champions and Reserve Champions brought several dollars per pound, but no one was buying. The Reserve Champion steer was on the block with the bid stalled at 65 cents per pound. We all were stunned. I went to Carl and said, "This is terrible. The Reserve Champion and the girl who raised it aren't getting more than market value." Carl agreed. His comment was, "Let's do something about it." We bid against each other until it sold for $1.50 per pound. Ever since, I have proudly displayed a picture of the Secretary of Agriculture, the 4-H girl, Carl, and I. Beside the picture on the wall is that steer's hide. Carl said that if I paid for the butchering, I could have the hide, and we split the meat.

Then came a sad time in Carl's life. The economy went into the cellar for the farmers and farming industry. Carl had to liquidate assets. Creditors were unkind, impatient, and forceful. I was elected to sell some of Carl's farms. This was tough for me because of our friendship. While Carl by far was not the only person in this position, he was the only one who was a gentleman in an unpleasant situation. I do mean a gentleman. He was very helpful, always pleasant, never resentful, and never bad-mouthed his enemies. That made it harder for me, emotionally, to handle the sale. But it wasn't long until Carl was back on top, buying livestock at 4-H and FFA sales. The most beautiful part of this story is that Carl and I were, and always will be, friends. We have many pleasant memories to share.

Last, but not least, no matter where we were amongst people, and whatever their stature may have been, and whether Carl was on the bottom or on the top, he always recognized me with a friendly hello and handshake. He made me feel as though I was a good friend of his, and that was important to me.

Shirley Brandt, Friend, Myerstown, Pa.

I came to know Carl and Margaret approximately 12 years ago when my husband and I began attending the Myerstown Church of the Brethren. Earl (my now deceased husband) had known Carl for many years prior to this, because he bought the majority of his farm equipment at Wenger's, where he was always treated right.

When my husband became terminally ill and the on- cologists had nothing more to offer, we were contemplating going to the Anderson Cancer Center in Texas for another opinion. When Carl got word of this, he called and told us to let him know when we were planning to go, and all the arrangements would be taken care of. It was so uplifting and heart-warming that anyone would provide such an offer at a time like that, when our hopes were shattered and our finances were drained.

Since that time, I have come to realize what a generous, caring person Carl really is. He has a passion for helping people and organizations, the young and the old. Many times, Carl is quietly in the background providing financial support but not having his name revealed.

Last year (2008), when I visited Carl in the hospital as he awaited his very critical operation, I told him I knew there were many people praying for him. He said, "I know. I told the sur- geons that I have people praying for me everywhere." And I'm sure he was right; they were praying everywhere! His frame of mind and attitude was so upbeat. He said, "Either way I win. I can't lose. It's a win-win situation." Yes, Carl is a true winner in so many ways, and I am so thankful to have him and Margaret as my friends.

Richard N. Darling, Friend, Orange City, Fla.

Some of the more memorable times I have spent with Carl have been highlighted by his philanthropy toward other people. Once while at the races in Daytona, Carl and I went out of the stands to get a pretzel from a vendor. As we approached, a woman, who had a disability, was standing just ahead of us. Out of the blue, Carl assisted her and then bought whatever she ordered out of the goodness of his heart.

Another time my wife, JoAnn, Carl, Margaret, and I were out to dinner. We had been in the restaurant for some time, when Margaret observed a large family, consisting of two adults and I believe six children. They all were sitting quietly, very well behaved, and obviously were not well to do. Margaret mentioned to Carl that they should buy their dinner. Without further ado, Carl bought their dinner. Carl truly believes that it is more blessed to give than to receive.

Carl is a people person. He gathers people from all over these United States through his magnetic personality, as well as business acquaintances. He forms pockets of people of varied occupations, who share a common interest and enjoys their camaraderie.

Clyde and Marian Deck, Friends, Lebanon, Pa.

I met Carl in 1947. The meeting place at the time was the Dixie Drive In. The attraction was girls bringing your orders and clamping the serving tray on your door. The gang consisted of local youth. Our group generally was Ralph Moyer, George Bowman, Ralph Sanger, Carl Reist, Ken Balmer, and Victor

Ziegler. I also went to more Sunday night church services than ever. Why? To meet girls! Carl had a 1949 black Oldsmobile. I was the only one with a 1947 Hudson. George Bowman and Carl Reist had Chevy Coupes.

Carl and I had many double dates, either going to the movies, bowling, or roller skating. Carl found Margaret and I met Marian, who later became our wives.

Carl started farming at Race Street, but soon found his passion in sales of farm machinery. I bought quite a few pieces of equipment when I started farming. Carl was one of the first people to fly with me when I started flying. I took him to sales, and this started my charter business.

I remember going out together after we were married and how Margaret could tell stories . . . a fun night! In later years we enjoyed family get-togethers and sharing different parenting issues. We are happy to have been a part of Carl and Margaret's family over the years! —Clyde

We had so many fun times with the Wengers. I'll just talk about two that took place around 1950. One Sunday afternoon after church, we decided to go find the Grand Canyon of Pennsylvania. We got back late that night. Though we never did get to the canyon, we had a great time! Another night we went to the theater in Reading to see a live show, featuring "Spike Jones and His Gang." The show was hilarious. We got silly and couldn't stop laughing. Laughter is the best medicine!
—Marian

George W. Dishong, Childhood Friend, Patent Attorney, Jaffrey, N.H.

Growing up, I lived in Number 9 Brick Row, maybe a block or so from where Carl lived upstairs in the Wenger's Store in

Rexmont. For a time I worked for his Uncle Myer Wenger, delivering more than 400 cases of milk as many as four mornings a week before school. I can remember going upstairs in the store and enjoying Carl's company and playing with many of his toys. He used to ride his bike to Myerstown to visit; Carl stayed very active.

I attended school with Carl at Cornwall but then, because I was poor, I went into the Navy. Carl started very quickly making his mark on the world with his business—known world-wide as a source of goods and services for any form of tractor. Later in life, Carl helped me pick a tractor to have at my home in Jaffrey, where Eva and I and many of the kids live. He even had it delivered to me from Myerstown. What a guy! We did get together a few times for class reunions and we did have some great parties in his and Margaret's beautiful stone farmhouse in Myerstown. I even remember him or one of the kids bringing a horse into the basement party room one time.

Anyway, best to Carl and the family.

Linda Dixon, Daytona International Speedway Employee, St. Augustine, Fla.

As an employee of the Daytona International Speedway, my contact with Mr. Wenger was his annual trip to Daytona for the races. I first met him while helping with his ticket purchases for the February races. He loved the races and came year after year.

The picture I see when I think of Carl Wenger is a man walking up to the counter in the Ticket Office at Daytona Speedway with a big hat and a bigger smile on his face, always carrying a large box of Pennsylvania pretzels. I thought for many years that he probably owned a pretzel company. He was always so happy to be at the races.

While Carl was in the hospital last year (2008), he called and said he would be having surgery the next day and was ready for whatever God had in store for him. He had a peace that few will ever experience.

Carl Wenger is a very caring man who loves his family and God.

Ann Doberstein, President of Reading Kubota, Fleetwood, Pa.

My heart often leads me to thoughts of Carl. I am president and manager of Reading Kubota—one of Wenger's sister companies. I had been in the equipment business for many years and really enjoyed the business and working with the Wenger family. Around 2003 my kids were very young and I was really struggling with the balance of being a good mom and running a demanding business. Carl and Margaret sat me down at lunch one day and we just talked. They shared stories about when they raised their kids. Carl spoke of the value in raising my kids in and around a family business—the kids seeing Fred and me working together in the business, serving our customers, and serving God and our community. Carl told me, "It's great to make money, but it's the friendships that will count at the end." I never forgot those words. And I will never forget those lunches to "just talk." Not many people today take the time to mentor young people. Carl and Margaret did that for me.

Jackie Dohner, Neighbor, Church Friend, Myerstown, Pa.

These memories and thoughts come to mind when I think of Carl Wenger:
• The signs that Carl put along the roads with the message

"Nice People Don't Litter." He is a person who cares about the land. We are glad to see the farmland across the street from our house and wonder what they will be planting this time.

• A person on the go and thinking of what might be done. In the fall he'll ask you if you want to buy any turkey tickets from the Lions Club. While my husband, Neal, is turkey hunting, I already got a turkey and it is delivered to our house. You can't beat that!

• A community minded man, interest in all.

Glenn and Shirley Eshelman, Friends, Strasburg, Pa.

We first became acquainted with Carl and Margaret when Carl gave us a phone call after a devastating fire burned the Sight & Sound Entertainment Centre in 1997. He was very concerned for us and invited us to join him and Margaret at a banquet. We felt very grateful that he would do this for us at such a difficult time in our life. We felt and experienced his love and concern for people right from the start. Since that time Carl and Margaret have been very dear friends to us. We have seen his compassionate heart in our lives and for others over and over again. He truly is a man who loves the Lord and his brothers and sisters in the Lord!

Glen Faus, former Executive Director of COBYS Family Services, Manheim, Pa.

After I retired from COBYS Family Services in 2001, my wife, Sheryl, and I received an invitation from Carl and Margaret to stay at their house in Florida for a few days. We called them with the dates that we could spend with them the following winter. Sheryl and I wanted to take some gifts along to let them know we appreciated their invitation. We thought they might appreciate some Shuey's Pretzels, from Lebanon. When we drove in the driveway of their Florida home, their garage door was open. And there, along the one side of the garage we saw a whole stack of boxes of Shuey's pretzels!

Carl was always "on the clock," always working. Carl and Margaret were showing Sheryl and me around the Daytona area one day and, as evening approached, Carl informed us that they would be taking us out for dinner. We were driving toward the restaurant they had chosen when, all of the sudden, Carl hit the brakes, veered off the road, and turned around. Margaret questioned what he was doing, and Carl told her that we just passed a place where they had a piece of farm equipment that he was looking to buy. Despite Margaret's protests, Carl drove back and in a short time purchased the piece of equipment, and we were soon on our way.

Another time I was visiting with Carl in his Myerstown office. Twice during the visit we were interrupted by phone calls. On the first call, Carl purchased a Minneapolis Moline tractor from a seller in one state. On the second call, he sold it to a buyer in another state.

Earl and June Forney, Church Friends, Ono, Pa.

I have had the privilege and pleasure of knowing Carl for about 60 years and consider him one of my outstanding friends. Carl is one of the most generous people I have known, as shown by his establishment of the Wenger Foundation, which benefits untold numbers of people. I have experienced his generosity many times on a personal level, when he would pick up our family's restaurant counter checks or invite me along with him for breakfast.

Although Carl built up a very impressive business empire (and at one point in the process experienced very difficult circumstances) Carl was always and still is the same "down to earth" congenial individual he's always been. My life and outlook on life have been positively impacted by my acquaintance with him.

As often has been said, and is very applicable in Carl and Margaret's case, is that behind every successful man there is an encouraging and supportive woman. Margaret fills and has filled that role superbly. We wish both of them life's very best.

P. Richard Forney, wife Verna, and Verna's Sister, Erlene, Friends, Myerstown, Pa.

I have been acquainted with Carl in various settings in past years. I was a classmate in elementary school. During those elementary years, I occasionally spent Saturdays visiting at Wenger's grocery store in Rexmont. I recognized that Carl had his chores and responsibilities at home as a youngster and throughout the days of his youth. His training during those years built the foundation for his life as a responsible adult.

Carl can easily be spotted by his big hat and spur of activity spawned by his contagious enthusiasm to correct or improve his communities and surroundings. He has been unselfish in sharing his business successes to support individuals as well as groups.

My father-in-law (Erlene and Verna's father), John Gibble, became a father figure and confidante to Carl after the death of his own father. As John Gibble helped out on the Wenger farms and businesses, a mutual respect developed. Upon John's death, Carl donated funds to the Myerstown Church of the Brethren, which were used by the family to purchase hand bells and the new blue Church of the Brethren hymnals as a memorial to John Gibble. Carl exemplifies loyalty to family and friends.

Danny Foster, Foster Bros. Equipment Company, Friend, Huntingdon, Tenn.

I have been in the farm equipment business in Huntingdon, Tennessee, for over 40 years. The first time I met Carl Wenger was in the 1980s at a sale in Ocilla, Georgia. We were both looking at an 886 International tractor. I noticed a knocking sound in the rear of the tractor when I drove it. A man standing on the ground said, "The rear end on that tractor is bad." When I got out of the tractor, Mr. Carl said, "There's nothing wrong with the rear end. It was just a loose wheel weight that was popping when the tractor moved." Mr. Carl and I both bid on the tractor and he got it bought. His honesty cost him money, because I wouldn't have bid on the tractor if he hadn't told me about the loose weight. But that's the way he is. We became good friends because of that incident and have remained so ever since then. I have enjoyed our relationship over the years and found his integrity to be beyond reproach. Thank you for your friendship, Mr. Carl.

Linda J. Gockley-Mohn, Friend, Denver, Pa.

My father, Jacob H. Gockley—a farm machinery dealer from Reinholds, Pennsylvania—and Carl Wenger go way back before I was born. They were both farm boys who also sold farm machinery and livestock and whatever. The Wengers were always a part of my parents' lives in business and friendship, and it was always a fun time to be had when we visited in Myerstown. A trip from our home in Reinholds to Myerstown was a big deal when I was a little girl. Unfortunately, the last times I saw Carl and Margaret was when my father died in 2003 and my mother died in January 2008. I wish my father was here to help you with this story. He was just as colorful as Carl and always filled with stories about things they did together. My own son recently had the pleasure of getting to know Carl.

In spring 2009, my son David Mohn was in the neighborhood buying parts for some heavy equipment, when he decided to stop in at Kumm Esse Diner in Myerstown for lunch. When he went inside to eat, an older man and lady came in, and my son recognized Carl immediately. (My father had David all over the place to do business with local farm machinery dealers when he was a little boy, so he knows all the good-old boys that his grandpa did business with.) Anyway, Carl looked at David and said, "I know you, but from where?" David proceeded to tell him he is Jake Gockley's grandson, and that was all it took. They had lunch together and told "Pop-Pop stories" and, as David went to leave, Carl bought him his lunch.

That meant so much to my son to hear stories about his grandfather and have his lunch bought by one of Pop-Pop's old buddies that he came home that night and called me to tell me all about it. It made me feel happy and brought back nice memories. As a few days passed, I just felt I needed to tell them how much this meant to David and me. So, I called Carl's daughter Rosie to share my thanks with her family. She invited me to come to their car show the following Saturday and see the Wenger family. Since my son has a few hot rods and antique vehicles I told her we would come up and bring along Uncle "Honey" (Elmer.) After a week's delay due to rain, David and his Uncle Honey headed for Myerstown in his model A pickup. (I did not feel well and needed to stay at home.) David and Honey and Carl hung out together and Carl even asked David to drive his prize car and tell him what is wrong with it. Then at the end of the night he asked David to park it in the garage for him. It was a tight squeeze but he got it in. David was once again so filled with Carl and Pop-Pop stories that he talked all weekend about Carl. My brother also really enjoyed himself, as Carl sat at the table with them and talked the night away.

Jim Henry, Friend and "Winter Pastor," Orlando, Fla.

We have many memories of Carl that cause our hearts to smile, but one of his most evident traits is generosity. He began attending our church, First Baptist, Orlando, several years ago, driving a good distance to be present. He and Margaret started inviting us for lunch or dinner at one of our or their favorite eateries. Toward the end of the meal, Carl would begin to talk about our church and its ministries and needs. Then he would turn to Margaret, apparently the treasurer of the marriage—or at least the bank—and receive a check. With pen in hand, he would quickly write out the check, making sure to whom it was to be given, and then fill in the amount. Carl would hand it over to me and say something like, "Take care of that for us." That was usually the dessert on the menu for us! With little fanfare, he would rise, put on the usual Stetson hat, and be off with a smile and a "Glad to do it" final word, leaving a smile on my face and in my heart. His heart is as large as his frame, and his compassion for the cause of Christ and people reflects his Lord's spirit.

Thomas A. Hess, Pastor, Painter, Friend, Bethel, Pa.

I'm a 66-year-old Mennonite pastor and painter. My initial acquaintance with Carl and Margaret Wenger came by way of Jubilee Ministries for a painting need Carl had at his tire re-pair shop in summer 2006. From the first, I appreciated Carl's humble commitment to relating to others and myself as equals, generally, and to recognize me as the "expert" in my work. He trusted me to give him the best job I knew how, and expressed sincere appreciation for a job well done. I felt quite honored when Carl took the time to give me a guided tour of the main Wenger Farm Machinery facilities and surrounding equipment yard, introducing me to various staff and family members and showing me how equipment is disassembled and parts sent out. I was further pleased for the prompt payment for my work and being given additional work to do later at the home farm where Carl and Margaret live.

Carl was admitted to the hospital during the time I was painting their house. The prognosis was serious, but Carl told me whatever happened he had peace about the outcome, whether that meant life or death. Afterward, while convalescing at home, he invited my wife and me to visit them, which we did. We had a lovely visit and fellowship. I was quite amazed at Carl's speedy recovery and adjustment to a radical change in diet. I see that as another evidence of Carl's implicit trust in the purpose and grace of God for all the variables of life.

Last fall, Carl said he was looking for a caretaker for his mountain cabin and wondered if I would be interested in, as he put it, "loving it" back to its potential. His son-in-law John P. Layser did the major repair work, while my wife and I painted, cleaned, landscaped, etc. I took the "loving it" as a go-ahead to be creative, hoping I was not presuming on Carl's trust in the final cost. I need not have worried for, again, Carl's response has been affirming and appreciative—a high honor from a man of his business stature and community influence.

Ron Hetrick, D.Ed., Friend, Fellow Rotarian, Palmyra, Pa.

Having served as a school administrator in the ELCO School District for 35 years, I had the pleasure of knowing Carl Wenger and his family for all of those years. Yet, I don't think I really knew Carl until I had an "up close and personal" encounter with him.

For many years, my face-to-face contacts with Carl were limited to weekly Rotary meetings and an occasional social interaction with him—and sometimes Margaret—at Rotary functions. Then, in 2003, Carl invited me to attend a National FFA Convention in Louisville, Kentucky, with his grandsons Adam and Jake. I really got to know Carl in many different ways on this trip.

I always knew about Carl's love and support for the Future Farmers of America, but on this trip I personally learned about the true value of participation in the FFA program and how this organization has been instrumental in helping youth grow into outstanding young adults. By being at his side throughout the convention, I discovered how Carl had supported this organization at the local, state, and national levels for many years.

Also, while on this trip, I learned about Carl's love for his family and his support for them through the years. The fact that he had established a business in which most of his family members work has always impressed me, but I didn't know much about the business. Being with him that week helped me to understand how the various parts of the business operate under the guidance of the various family members. It was most interesting to hear him describe with pride how each member of his family contributes to the success of the business by carrying out their individual responsibilities. I had a greater understanding of the business after that week and felt I got to know more about the members of his family, who I had known only casually before.

My understanding of Carl Wenger as a philanthropist also increased during the week I spent with him. Carl is a generous supporter of so many worthy groups through the foundation that he established to give back to the community. I learned that Carl is a "giver" and takes great pleasure in being able to share his good fortune in life with others. I was personally the recipient of his generosity several times, and the Eastern Lebanon County Schools and students benefitted from the Wenger Foundation at various times. The district and I will be ever grateful for Carl Wenger's gifts.

May both Carl and Margaret be the recipients of many years of health and happiness as a reward for what they have given to help others achieve.

Brian H. Hoffman, Road Foreman, Jackson Township, Myerstown, Pa.

I met Carl through his family. I went to school with his daughters and sons, and I'm friends of all. I met Carl on several occasions throughout my lifetime. He was always there if I needed anything and he was willing to help anyone else if called upon. His sons always have helped me in my need of equipment for either professional or personal use. With that being said, I would do my best to help him or them in any way that I could. Over the years we have worked on many projects for Carl, either the Township or for the betterment of the community. One of Carl's goals was to get areas of weeds that needed to be cut. He would say, "I will supply a tractor and you do the operating," and I complied. This took place throughout Jackson Township and in the Borough of Myerstown. His sons would say, "What did Carl rope you into this time?" And so I would tell them.

I have a love for old cars and trucks, and so does Carl. He asked me one time to get his Oldsmobile out and wash and wax it, take it for a drive, bring it back, and put it away for next time. And so I did! Since that time I had known he had some old trucks that he bought at sales throughout the years and had kept in storage. One day I went and asked him if he wanted to sell any of them. His reply was, "WHO WANTS TO KNOW?" I said I was interested in one of them. He said that he only had one left and that he wanted to keep it. However, he asked if I would help him get the truck running again, since it had been sitting for about 20 years. AND SO I DID.

In the meantime, Carl had become ill and spent many weeks in the hospital. I had just restored the truck to road worthiness shortly after his return home from the hospital. I stopped in to visit, and asked him if he was up to a ride in his truck. He said he was, and so we went for a ride. The expression on his face was—well, let's just say the timing was perfect. To come home from the hospital was one good thing, and to ride in his truck was another. During his illness he may not have expected to ever do either one. Thanks for your friendship, Carl!

Roger Jeremiah, Business Associate, Friend, Myerstown, Pa.

I have known Carl in a business setting on and off for most of the 30 years I have spent here in Dutch country. I have many fond memories of Carl, such as the first time I watched him eat a whole lemon, up to and including the lament he expressed when "the home" on Railroad Street was closed by the State and how disappointed he was that no one had asked for his help to keep it open. Most of my memories, however, are not of events but rather of my interactions with Carl that have helped me to understand his character. Carl has a good sense of God's purpose for his life. He truly is a good man and I don't know very many of those! Whether we realize it or not, all of us who know Carl have been blessed. Hopefully, those blessings will continue long into the future. I know in my case, it won't take a book to remind me. Carl, just keep on being you for as long as you can.

David Keller, Friend, Business Associate, Myerstown, Pa.

My acquaintance with Carl goes back to our membership in the Midway Church of the Brethren. We both sold tractors, so that put us in a business relationship. In recent years we have gotten together for lunch several times. I enjoyed the "tractor talk" and the tours I was given of the Wenger business. We both experienced that working together is better than competing with each other. Carl has a heart of generosity and helping others. I am grateful for the good relationship we have.

Deena Kent, Friend, Business Associate, Orange City, Fla.

I first met the Wengers when I was a teenager in the late '80s, just after my father, Bob Pelland, started to do business with Mr. Wenger. Every summer my family would drive to Massachusetts and Rhode Island. One summer on the way through Pennsylvania we stayed at the Wengers' cabin on the mountainside. I only remember parts of it, but I do remember how beautiful the cabin was, and the view was just breathtaking.

They took us through Amish country, the Hershey factory, to watch Carl's son Davey race, and I spent some time with a few of their grandchildren. I thoroughly enjoyed my time during that summer, and I had made a new friend.

Within a few years, Renee—the granddaughter that I had the most in common with—had her life tragically taken. It was shortly after that when I realized how much Mr. Wenger was motivated to help others. He started a foundation in her memory and helps with other foundations as well. The Wengers' endless hospitality and unselfishness is unbelievable. As an adult, I would like to say, "Thank you for your friendship over the years to our family." To Mrs. Wenger, I say, "Hands down, you run the best bed and breakfast in town!"

Jeff King, Development Director, Rodeheaver Boys Ranch, Palatka, Fla.

I first became associated with Carl Wenger in July 2001, shortly after becoming Development Director for the Rodeheaver Boys Ranch. The occasion was our annual public auction to benefit the Ranch. I noticed during the event that Carl was buying several items.

It was his handling of a piano that endeared my wife and me to Carl. It was an old antique piano, and Donna was bidding against Carl and another gentleman. The bid went up above what my wife was able to afford, so she dropped out of the bidding. Carl went on to outbid the other gentleman. Later, Carl came over to my wife and asked some questions about why she wanted the piano. Donna explained that it was for her mother, who had played piano when Donna was young. Her mother mentioned that she would love to play again, but could not afford to buy another piano. Carl then gave Donna a piece of the piano keyboard that was loose and told her that he bought the piano for her. Donna and I both were moved to tears by his gesture, and we have been close friends ever since.

Carl and Margaret have both made major impacts on the boys and Ranch staff. They have been significant donors and they especially enjoy bidding up the hogs being sold by the Ranch boys at the annual Putnam County Fair.

Carl Wenger is a man who loves people and loves to make others happy . . . especially those who are hurting. Carl is a man who truly practices what he believes and the boys who live at Rodeheaver Boys Ranch have better lives because of the investments he has made.

John B. Kline, Executive Director, On-Fire Youth Ministry Inc., Myerstown, Pa.

My experiences with Carl began when I, at age 12, accompanied my father to tractor sales at Carl's facility in Myerstown. They used to drive the tractors through one of the buildings at the dealership on Race Street to be auctioned. On a cold winter night, Carl asked if I would put the overhead door up and down, as tractors entered and exited the building. My dad went home around 9:00 that night, and Carl took me home later after the sale. I distinctly remember him telling me that I did a good job, and he gave me $20.

In 1983 I was selected FFA Eastern Region Star Farmer of America, making me a candidate for Star Farmer of America. At the same time, Carl and Margaret's son Glenn was running for a national FFA office. The selection of Star Farmer would take place in Kansas City, but my father's unwillingness to fly in an airplane would prevent his attendance. Carl tracked down my dad, who was working on a tractor out in a field south of Schaefferstown. In a fashion unique to Carl alone, he said to my dad, "Norman, our sons are going to be on the stage in Kansas City and we should be there." Not one to take no for an answer, Carl had already purchased the airfare and reserved the motel rooms for he and Margaret, as well as my mom and dad. To my surprise, my parents joined me in Kansas City. What a blessed memory that was to me at a young, impressionable age of 21 years old.

In more recent years Carl and Margaret's generosity has continued to influence young men and women through the work of On-Fire Youth Ministry in Myerstown. Through financial support, advocacy, assisting me in contacts, and just teaching me to think outside the box, their partnership has allowed our ministry to grow tremendously over the past 20 years. More teens have been impacted due to the influence of the Wenger family, The

Wenger Foundation Praise Dinner event, and countless other wonderful people in this magnificent community!

Verna Kline, Friend, Myerstown, Pa.

Back in 1981, our son John and Carl's son Glenn graduated together from ELCO High School, where both boys were very active in the FFA. They were traveling to Kansas City, Missouri, for the National FFA Convention in 1983, as Glenn was running for a national FFA office and John was Eastern Region Star Farmer and in the running for Star Farmer of America. We had never attended the convention and had no plans to this year.

One day, John's father was several miles from home in the fields and Carl came to visit. Carl said, "Norman, our boys are out at the convention to be recognized for special awards and we are not there." Norman was never in an airplane and always declared he would never fly, but it was too late to drive. After several minutes of encouraging him, Norman agreed to go. We did make the trip with Carl and Margaret and got to see the boys receive their awards. Due to a good flying experience, Norman went with my brother Victor Ziegler to Puerto Rico in spring 1984, and that fall we traveled with another couple to Europe for two weeks and saw many things, including the Passion Play at Oberammergau. Norman flew several other times within our country. I thank Carl for the encouragement he gave to Norman, which allowed us to enjoy many good experiences together. I also thank God for friends like Carl and Margaret. Norman made his last flight in February 2006 to his eternal home.

Donald Klopp, Friend, Bethel, Pa.

It was right after World War II, in the 1940s, that I met Carl. We were in our late teens. A lot of challenges were being presented to young people at that time. Carl introduced me to quite a few of his friends, and they became my friends also. He wasn't involved with anyone that was scruffy. There was no boozing or drugs. We had a lot of good times running around together.

I am reminded periodically by an old friend from Womelsdorf about the time I left him stranded on a corner in Myerstown. If Carl hadn't come along, he says he would have been there until the next day, but Carl took him home and never said a word about it to me. (There must have been a girl involved.)

There are friends, and then there are *friends*, and Carl was a *friend*, and is to this day after all these years. We were not lily white, but had little shades of grey in us. Though we don't see each other too often anymore, when we meet the old friendship rekindles. I love him like a brother.

Craig N. Kreider, Relative, Petersburg, Pa.

Carl was always involved with farm youth. He strongly supported FFA, hosting FFA officers during state conferences. He also supported youth livestock sales throughout the state. A number of years ago he contacted me to buy livestock at our county youth sale in Huntingdon County because he was involved with a youth sale elsewhere in the state.

Carl was always a generous host. When my parents first went to Florida, looking for an area to resettle in retirement, Carl had them stay for days while they showed them around. My father told me how Carl was always taking friends out to dinner.

Landis Kupp, Friend, Lebanon, Pa.

I have known Carl all of my lifetime. Carl has always been a people person and always willing to do things for the community. Carl and I flew several times to Florida to attend auctions and stay in his DeLand home. These trips always proved to be very interesting. I was also involved in helping to restore Carl's '49 Olds. (Carl owns a '49 Oldsmobile that is almost an exact replica of his first car.)

Ed and Sherrie Liskey, Friends, Myerstown, Pa.

We have known Carl for many years. He is a very active member of the Myerstown Church of the Brethren, where we attend. We personally felt his generosity to our family a few years ago. Our middle son, Sean, was hired by Wengers of Myerstown while he was in high school and continued to work there after he graduated. He would come home and tell us fondly, "C.W. worked with us today," or "C.W. came in the shop to say hello to the guys today."

In 2004, Sean was diagnosed with a cancerous brain tumor. As he went through surgery, radiation, and chemo treatments, Wengers kept him on at work, and they were very supportive. Our church youth group had fund raisers for Sean, and the Wenger Foundation agreed to match the amount raised. It turned out to be a significant amount of money for Sean.

As Sean's condition got worse and he had a difficult time doing his job, Wengers kept him on as long as they could. Sean went to live with the Lord on January 27, 2008, at the age of 29.

Carl and his family have been a special blessing to Sean and us. We are eternally grateful and will never forget his kindness. Carl is a wonderful man.

Donald Martin, Friend, Former Owner Martin's Tractor Equipment, Casselberry, Fla.

The first time I met Carl was at an auction in Charlotte, N.C., in the late 1970s. I was having a good day buying tractors. My business was going real good at that time. I think Carl thought it was too, so he introduced himself. We became friends at that time.

Carl asked me why I was doing good at that time. I told him I believed it was the Lord, and I went to church and that I tithed with what the Lord allowed me to have. I think that was one thing that Carl was wondering.

Ever since then, my wife, Nancy, and I and Carl and Margaret have been good friends. We have visited in each other's homes. Through the many years we have had a lot of dealings and a great relationship.

Dawson McAllister, Youth Communicator, Radio Personality, Columbia, Tenn.

Well, I love Carl Wenger. He and I have been friends for the last couple of years. I remember not too long ago I spent a whole day with him. What he did was he just took me around and showed me all the different companies that he had started, and what they were doing, and how he got to be where he was, the common sense that he had learned from his father. One thing I noticed about Carl when he showed me all these things—and it took quite a while—I didn't hear any ego at all in his voice. I didn't hear anything but, "God has done this. God has done that." You know, and he means it. He's got the answer to life, because you can build all the things in the world you want, but in the end you leave them all behind. The question is, Why did you do it? Why did you build what you built?

Why these companies? And what are you going to leave behind? What legacy? And what will matter for eternity? That's what Carl's all about, leaving a legacy and what matters for eternity. God just gifted this man with brilliant business sense, and common sense, and commitment to his customers, and here he is today leaving a legacy and doing what matters for eternity. Love ya', Carl.

Al Miller, Ag Industrial, Friend, Northeast, Md.

Carl has been a friend and mentor to me. I got to know Carl shortly after Wenger's bought our company in 1994. He always made me feel welcome in the Wenger organization and always was there for me to answer any questions or to just listen to me. Carl told me that there were really no competitors in this business, only opportunities for new customers. As a young dairy farmer, I was a member of a very close family and a close farm community. We always tried to help the neighbors get the job done and worked together toward that end. Carl ran his business the same way, which was very refreshing for me.

Advice from Carl always came along when I least expected it, but I later found it to be near perfect timing. One day at the Cecil County Fair, just before the 4-H Livestock Sale, Carl happened to mention to me that the other day he had gotten upset with a person. He told me that he was never going to do that again, because the only one it hurt was him. He said the guy wasn't affected by his anger, but it had bothered Carl. Carl had trouble sleeping that night and, at that point, he knew that it was definitely not worth getting upset about—how profound! Just think about that for a bit and you will realize how true that statement is and always will be. A couple of days later, I relayed that story to my minister who speaks on that subject very often. I have also shared that with my men's group at church. I will never forget that getting upset and angry does more harm to me than the other guy.

A few years ago, we had a very good year at Ag Industrial. As a result, we donated a substantial amount of money to our local church toward their building fund. I had mentioned that to Carl and he was immediately very happy about our decision. He proceeded to tell me how the Wenger family had done that for years, and that their success was faith-based. They always seem to glean more from their gifts than they actually gave. My father had always said that same thing to me, growing up: Little effort equals little reward, and doing something nice for someone always was rewarded well. When my youngest son, Rob, was in middle school, I used to always say to him, "Go out and do something nice for someone today."

Carl has taught me a lot about life over the years—not only how to make money, but also to share that wealth. He is a great motivator, challenging us to be the best we can be. I think the greatest compliment one man can give to another is that you think he is a "disciple of God." Carl Wenger is a true disciple of God.

Dave Miller, DVM (Retired), Friend, DeLand, Fla.

I'm a retired veterinarian and old farm boy from Ohio. I live year round in Florida about a mile from the Wengers' winter home in DeLand. I first met Carl about seven or eight years ago when he walked into a farm toy show in DeLand, where I was displaying. In a brief conversation we learned that we were almost neighbors and that he also was the father of Lloyd Wenger, a farm toy collector of some renown. In addition, I learned they operate Wengers of Myerstown. Anyone who has met Carl knows it doesn't take long to learn about him. Before the day was over, he brought friends over to see my collection of model farm toys. We have been friends ever since.

Carl introduced me to southern farm machinery auctions and NASCAR racing. While living only 20 miles from the Daytona track, I always said I wouldn't go to the races unless I had a good seat and someone else drove. Well, Carl came through on both counts. He always drove, he had a good parking place at Friendly's Restaurant, just across the street from the track, and he always had tickets for good seats. Had it not been for Carl, I probably never would have gone to Daytona to the races.

Shortly after meeting Carl, he asked me if I wanted to go to an auction with him. It may have been in Ocala or somewhere in Georgia. I met Carl at his house early to ride with him. Margaret was up and had Carl all ready to go. She told me that she was sure glad that I—and not her—was going with him because she was getting tired and too old to climb up on tractors to get hour meter readings, etc. I went to quite a few auctions with Carl and, while I'm only four years younger than Carl, it was always my job to do the climbing to get the necessary information.

Carl has been in business for 50 years or more, and he loves the machinery auction and tractor shows. If you travel these events with Carl, you soon learn how many friends he has. I think that Western hat is his trademark, easily recognized. Every few minutes someone will shout out, "Hey Wenger!" Then we stop to let Carl visit.

Carl is a very honest person. He is "true and loyal" to his religion, family, and friends. His philanthropic efforts go beyond those of the average person and demonstrate his commitment to better his community and mankind. I continue to value Carl's friendship.

Randy and Barbara Miller, Friends, Myerstown, Pa.

We came to know Carl through the Myerstown-ELCO Rotary Club. We both went to school with some of Carl's children, but when Barbara had her auto accident on September 18, 2001, we soon learned how kind, giving, and generous a person Carl is. After all the trials Carl, Margaret and their family have encountered, he and Margaret still remain true believers in God. They are always there to lend a hand to those in need.

Bud and Joyce Mitstifer, Friends, Myerstown, Pa.

Carl and Margaret, WOW what friends! We have known the Wengers for over 30 years. As we get older we get much more attached to the friendship we share.

Carl is a strong General Motors man and I am a Ford man. I tell him now that the world situation is what it is he can see why I stick to Fords. We poke fun at one another all the time and still laugh about it. (Boy, has he got his family brainwashed the same way.)

Carl's love for people shows in so many ways. He is always trying to help someone or their family, with the love of the Lord always being in the back of his mind. And he does not preach it to you; it comes out in a very loving way to anyone who will listen.

Carl loves to go racing at Daytona, and he takes his time to get the tickets for all the group and does it with enjoyment. We have to pay him for our tickets, but he makes no profit. If you happen to sit next to him, however, he takes up half your seat, but gives you no refund for the half he uses. We all have a good time and look forward to going racing again in the coming year. Now that Carl has lost so much weight, he won't need to take part of my seat! After the race it's off to Friendly's restaurant for another meal. In fact, some days we eat three meals there. We all love to go to Friendly's in Daytona, and Carl loves to get a hug from the waitress that has known him for many years. (Actually, I enjoy that myself.)

Carl sells turkeys for the Lions Club, and we all help him to achieve his goal, which keeps increasing each year. Knowing Carl and Margaret has been a blessing sent to us in our lives, so much so that we bought a home in Florida a short distance away from them. Now we can go to Dairy Queen in Pennsylvania or McDonalds when in the south for a sundae with the Wengers. Carl is a wonderful friend and we truly love his friendship.

I could go on and on with many stories, but someone else will fill in, I am sure. And by the way, no one in God's green earth knows as much about farm tractors as Carl Wenger!

Dean O. Moyer, Chairman, Jackson Township Supervisors, Myerstown, Pa.

When I moved to Myerstown from Port Carbon, Pennsylvania, in 1960, everyone I met was a new acquaintance, including Carl. However, as time went by, I would see this big man with the western boots and large cowboy hat in the area. When I inquired who this was, I was told he was Carl Wenger, owner of Wenger's Farm Machinery. I had several brothers who were farming in the area and purchased parts from Carl's business, thus making Carl's name and type of business more accessible to me.

I joined the Myerstown Lions Club in 1977, where I was introduced to Carl as a longtime member of the club. While my wife, Janie, and I never traveled or had a personal relationship with Carl and Margaret, our knowledge of the Wengers was expanded through the many projects that this very God-driven couple sponsored or supported.

One project that stands out is the Praise Dinner, held each spring at the Lebanon Expo Center. Another is the Myerstown Lions Club's turkey sale, held each November. One year I remember Carl single-handedly sold approximately 550 turkeys—almost a $5,000.00 profit for our club. I believe the rest of us sold a total of about 50 turkeys.

As chairman of the Jackson Township Board of Supervisors, I always have been able to rely on Carl to help us. If we needed a particular piece of equipment for a special project, Wenger's never let us down, providing what we needed at no cost to the Township.

As a very committed Christian and family man and wife, Carl and Margaret passed many positive attributes on to their children, grandchildren, and great-grandchildren, assuring that their legacy will continue long into the future. Thank you, Carl and Margaret, for making the lives of everyone in your extended family a true blessing.

God bless both of you and a sincere thank you for making our lives so much better by just knowing you.

George E. Patton Jr., Longtime Friend, Lebanon, Pa.

Knowing Carl for more than 40 years—both socially and as a fellow club member—has made us very good friends. A word I would use to describe Carl is "dedication." He is dedicated to family, church, business, civic responsibility, and to a multitude of friends.

I share two similar life-changing memories with Carl. First, was the proud occasion when his son Glenn was an FFA Eastern Regional Star Agri-Business award winner (1982-83). Two years earlier (1980-81), my daughter was selected as Miss Pennsylvania and represented the state in the Miss America Pageant. We both were proud fathers and shared many pleasant memories. Second was tragedy that we shared: Carl lost a granddaughter in 1994 and I lost a 16-year-old grandson in 2005, killed by a drunk driver.

Our pleasant memories include Carl selling and delivering frozen turkeys for his civic club at Thanksgiving, always wearing his cowboy hat and big belt buckle. We had many conversations over the years about auto racing, family situations, and business problems, and we just enjoyed each other's company.

Carl is always available to give a word of advice, encouragement, or sympathy. I admire his business acumen and how he has been able to incorporate his sons and daughters into his operations. I was also a product of a family business and learned that it is not easy to work for your father. He has established a great relationship.

His Christian philosophy is to be admired in this day and age. He is generous to a fault, which is found by his contributions to church and community. It is my privilege to have known Carl for these many years, and I am proud to have him as a good friend.

Mr. and Mrs. Robert Pelland, Owners West Volusia Shed Company, Orange City, Fla.

We met Carl in the 1980s, when he stopped in one day at our place of business to purchase a utility building. After a year or so had passed, he stopped in and wondered if we would sell some of his implements. Since then, we have done business and have been close friends with Carl and Margaret. About 10 years ago, as we were dining out with them, the Wengers suggested that we go see a nearby gospel show. We attended that show, not knowing if we would enjoy this new experience. It was one of the best shows that we ever attended. Thanks, Carl and Margaret, for introducing us to gospel music. We have been going yearly to see Bill Gaither's Homecoming in Orlando ever since. Just two words to describe Carl and Margaret: GREAT PEOPLE to have as friends.

Leonard Raub, Friend, Womelsdorf, Pa.

I have known Carl Wenger for a number of years as a businessman and a great giver to those who have a need. Back in 1999, God's Missionary Church in Lebanon, Pennsylvania, had begun a huge building program, with volunteers performing much of the labor. I contacted Carl and asked if we could rent equipment from Wengers of Myerstown. Instead, he graciously donated any piece of equipment we needed for the next four years. Wengers would bring an excavator, roller, or bulldozer for us to use. Soon they would sell that piece and bring us another one. It happened many times with almost every type of equipment they lent us. I believe God blessed them for their kindness, which we deeply appreciated

About three years ago I got word Carl was in serious physical condition. I heard about it in church one Sunday morning, and I immediately went to Good Samaritan Hospital in Lebanon to see Carl. We found him in the lobby, talking with many of his friends. He began to share about the seriousness of his physical problems. I remember Carl was unsure whether he would be with us much longer. We talked for a while, and I asked if I could have prayer with him. He agreed. When we prayed I felt the Lord heard us. Thank the Lord, Carl came through the operation with flying colors. I visited Carl in the hospital, and our friendship became very close. Today we visit him in Pennsylvania and in Florida. Thanks, Carl, for all you have done for the work of God!

Donald and Helen Reinford, Friends, Lebanon, Pa.

We met Carl and Margaret many years ago when we were looking for a church to worship at that had good teaching, music programs, and caring people. We found that at Midway

Church of the Brethren, near Lebanon, where Carl and Margaret worshipped.

They introduced us to oriental cuisine, and we shared many a Sunday meal at a little Chinese restaurant on North Lincoln Avenue in Lebanon. It was interesting to us that the owner recognized Carl and Margaret as regular customers.

We found that they had a genuine, caring attitude about anything they were involved in, and they gave it their all. As you may have noticed, I always refer to "Carl and Margaret," and that is just as it should be. They are a team. In February 2006, we had plans to visit them in Florida on our way home. Carl called to ask if we could arrive by 4 p.m. He wanted us to go along to a recognition dinner for a piece of equipment that Wengers of Myerstown had donated for a small church's disaster relief mission. After a delicious meal, they presented Carl with a plaque in appreciation for the truck. He was so concerned that Margaret should have had her name on the plaque because "she did most of the work, made most of the arrangements."

We have always enjoyed the Praise Dinner and the financial support that goes to the needy groups. They are a true blessing to many!

Len and Marian Schott, Friends, Myerstown, Pa.

My first recollection of Carl Wenger goes back to our high school days at Myerstown High School. In those days, only a few had a car, and Carl was one who did. I think it was then that he was first called a "cowboy." I lived in Myerstown at the corner of Main and College Streets. When we would hear the tires squeal from "digging out" at the stop sign, we would ask, "Who was that?" The answer was, "Oh, it's that cowboy, Carl Wenger."

Carl started in business at a young age and with the same enthusiasm and "cowboy spirit" as he drove those powerful cars. He achieved the American dream by working long and hard. Through persistence and determination, he saw his way through the good times and bad to the success we recognize today in Wengers of Myerstown and associated businesses.

He would be the first to admit that this was possible only with the support and hard work of his wife, Margaret, and his fine children, employees, and many friends and other businessmen of the area.

What makes people special is how they share their success with their community and beyond. Carl has given so much financially and through physical effort that we cannot begin to fathom how far-reaching his generosity has benefitted and will continue to benefit others.

At the 2009 Wenger Foundation Praise Dinner, speaker Ken Gaub said, "Our purpose here is to help others." Well, Carl, my friend, you certainly have done that. Happy trails!

Hilda Schuler, Friend, Cairo, Ga.

I have known Carl Wenger for many years. My husband, Ronald, also lived in Pennsylvania—in the Kutztown area from 1959 to 1967. During this time we got to know Wenger's Machinery Company because my husband bought and sold tractors and equipment and got some parts from the Wengers. I didn't personally meet Carl until years later, sometime in the 1980s.

We had moved to a 400-tree pecan farm in Cairo, GA, in 1967, and my husband also operated a farm machinery business. We would see Carl at Weeks Auction Company in Moultrie, GA, where he came every month to buy tractors and equipment. One time, a customer needed a Ford Loader Backhoe, but didn't have the money to buy one. Carl had just bought one. Ron asked Carl if we could take it to our place, 45 minutes away, fix up a few things on it, and try to sell it to our customer. If it didn't sell, we would bring it back to the next month's auction. Carl agreed to this arrangement and said that we would split the profit after expenses. So started a long many years of working with Carl on equipment. It worked real well for both of us.

Around 1985 three hurricanes came through our area and devastated our pecan crop. This put us into a financial bind. Our 60-acre farm was going to be foreclosed on, and Carl again came to the rescue. We later turned this into a subdivision and, when Ron died in 2000, Carl bought the subdivision. I still mow and take care of it.

Carl has been a real, true friend over the years and still is to this day. His word is true. It's like signing a contract. If he tells you something, he will do it. Like the old saying, "They don't make them like that anymore."

I like Carl's philosophy: "If you can't say something good about a person, don't say it."

And, of course, we can't forget Margaret. She has stood by him all these years. Again the saying, "Behind every successful man is a good woman."

Mr. and Mrs. Frederick (Fritz) Shaak, Neighbor, Myerstown, Pa.

Carl and Margaret Wenger have been our neighbors for almost 50 years. Their children and our children and grandchildren have always been friends. The neighborhood has been busy and action-filled. We have shared many joyful times and a few sad ones, but there has never been a conflict. There has never been an unkind word. The Wengers are wonderful neighbors.

The Wenger farm is beautiful. The field across the street from our home gives us pleasure and helps us celebrate the seasons as we watch the plowing, planting, and harvesting of crops.

The scene northeast of our home is magnificent. We see their lovely home, the creek, and the pasture with the British White Park Cattle grazing. The town, church steeples, mountains, and then the sky complete the picture. Thanks to Carl, we enjoy this unmatched picture of beauty daily.

Carl, Margaret, and their family have enriched our lives and the lives of our family. It has been a blessing to have them as friends and neighbors.

Martha Shaak, Friend, Former Camp Swatara Development Representative, Palmyra, Pa.

When someone mentions Carl Wenger, my husband, Dennis, and I immediately picture a big smile, outgoing manner, and a cowboy hat. The contrast with Margaret's more quiet style is dramatic, until she mentions that watching bull riding is one of her favorite forms of entertainment. From there, conversation explodes into the realm of good "Brethren" FUN. Gracious hospitality and delightful conversation are always part of a gathering with Carl and Margaret. One thing is certain, gracious hospitality embraces the many within their circle of friends; their ministry of generosity simply overflows toward the Church of the Brethren and the needs of their surrounding community. "Who is my neighbor?"—as the parable asks—is defined by Carl liberally and inclusively. Generosity flows from his heart of hospitality.

Carl is always a dynamic presence at the Brethren Disaster Relief Auctions. One might call him a cheerleader for the auction mission, all the while greeting and enjoying conversation with those around him. On occasion, I have heard him kindly challenge a brother or sister to increase their bid. And I wonder how many times it was Carl who said, "Sell it again."

One of our interactions with Carl and Margaret that we recall with great fondness took place a number of years ago.

We were doing lead gift visits for a capital campaign to benefit Camp Swatara. I called for an appointment to meet with Carl and Margaret. He responded by inviting us to a lovely meal at the Quentin Riding Club to enjoy the stewardship moment with us in a spirit of celebration. Carl and Margaret gave generously to the campaign, personally and through the Wenger Foundation. Carl took the art of giving so seriously that he made it fun for himself and for those who were in the position of asking. He seemed to understand intuitively that charitable acts begin with relationships, and Carl is very comfortable relating to many different persons.

The idea of fundraising with a foundation for the benefit of the community was a new idea for us. But knowing Carl and his family who comprise the Wenger Foundation, it was easy to see the connection between a fun night out at a Wenger Foundation Praise Dinner and encouraging others to be likewise generous. We commend the way this has worked for the many ministries that have been supported through the work of the Wenger Foundation. We applaud the initiative to begin and fund such an endeavor, and we are deeply appreciative of Carl, who lives life in such a positive, life-affirming way.

My husband and I are honored to pay tribute to Carl and Margaret Wenger for their outstanding example of hospitality, their generosity of heart in giving to many different community and denominational ministries, and their ebullience of spirit that is contagious and God-bearing. We learned to know Carl and Margaret through their ministry of philanthropy; we became friends in the process. That is a gift in itself.

Thomas A. Sherk, Distant Relative, Friend, Lebanon, Pa.

During the past year, I have had the wonderful opportunity to spend some time with Margaret and Carl Wenger. They truly represent values that embody people of the Christian faith. Through their dedication, work ethic, and skills, their various business ventures have been very successful by any standard. They both have made a commitment to share their good fortune with organizations and people in need through the Wenger Foundation. I have witnessed countless examples of their generosity and commitment to making our world a better place for all people.

While in their company, I sense a deep, meaningful, and loving relationship that Margaret and Carl have together. Margaret's stories about Carl are funny and reveal a complex character. Carl has a style and grace unique to a person of his abilities. He is down to earth, friendly, and treats all people with respect.

Carl and Margaret have had a positive influence on me and have changed my way of thinking about life through their actions. I consider it an honor to know both of them and hope they will remain in good health so that they may continue to enrich those whose lives they touch.

Thomas Smith, Friend, Watervliet, Mich.

My relationship with Carl and Margaret Wenger has been for a relatively short period of time—roughly three years. From the beginning, they both impressed us as being loving, giving, and devout Christians. We believe they have a strong philosophy of making this a better world by sharing and giving to others, and that they will always practice this philosophy during their lifetime. My wife, Verna, and I will always be thankful for having met these wonderful people and look forward to many more years of friendship. God bless them.

Roger Sorensen, Friend, Farm Equipment Dealer, Harlan, Iowa

Carl is a Christian man who loves his God. He wants to treat his friends and customers fair. He has also made this known to his sons and employees. Carl is known as a guy who would rather give you something than have you give him something. Here are some of his quotes:

"If what you are doing is working, keep doing it. Don't change your game plan if it is working."

"The Wenger Way."

I found this statement on Carl's business card: "It's not what you gain but what you give that measures the worth of the life you live."

We have been with Carl to the races a number of times in Daytona. One of his favorite places to eat and meet is at Friendly's across from the race track.

Carl has made a big impact on my life and has given me many words of wisdom when I have called him and asked for advice. Carl gives credit for much of his success to his wife, Margaret.

Jerome "Jerry" Spangler, Friend Since High School, Myerstown, Pa.

Carl and I have always been great friends. What more can I say about a great person like Carl and his wonderful wife and great family. There is nothing he wouldn't do for you.

Milt Stoltzfus, Friendship Community, Friend and Recipient of Carl's Generosity, Lititz, Pa.

Carl Wenger is a man who has chosen to use the blessings that have been shared with him to touch the lives of others. As a successful businessman, Carl has modeled to his family the privilege of affecting many ministries and others in the local community with his generosity.

At Friendship Community, our relationship with Carl began in 2000 as Friendship Community expanded its services for people with developmental disabilities into Lebanon County. Carl was on our list of businessmen to visit. I remember the first time I saw Carl with his cowboy hat and large presence—I wondered if he was an approachable man or if he liked to keep his distance from those around him.

In our first meeting, Carl listened to our story without offering an indication to me as to what he was thinking. As the subject of financial support was mentioned, Carl offered the invitation that would change our relationship. Although he was not prepared to give an outright gift, he wondered if we would be open to be a part of an event called "The Praise Dinner," which was a family-organized fundraising event to benefit several local ministries. Our willingness to say yes and the openness of Carl and his family to extend the invitation to us brought to us the example of the community working together—which I believe is an example of how Carl thinks. Rather than one person doing all the work, extend the invitation for many to gather around and help each other.

We soon learned that Carl was approachable and was deeply interested in our ministry and the people served. His gift to us has been an openness to offer friendship, advice, and a belief in the power of community.

David A. Swanger, Childhood Neighbor, Dover, Pa.

It was about 1940 when my parents moved to 431 S. Race Street, next to the Wenger farm in Myerstown. At two years of age, I was too young to know Carl or anything about him. But by about 1948, stories were many about the farm life next door. During the wheat harvesting, I was told, Carl preferred to drive the tractor. My older brother Harold was a classmate of Carl's at Myerstown High School. Close to graduation time, Carl's dad bought him a black 1949 Oldsmobile as a graduation present.

George Swanger, Childhood Neighbor, Newmanstown, Pa.

I was born in 1950, the year Carl graduated from high school. My oldest brother is a classmate of Carl's. It was also in 1950 that the Wenger family business got going. From my earliest recollections, there was always something going on at the Wenger house. Dairy farming under the watchful eye of John Wenger was what kept things going. Carl did not seem to take to that endeavor. He was more into buying and selling. "Buy low, sell high." He would buy repairable machinery, refurbish it, and make a profit selling it.

The Wenger garage was always full of tractors in various states of repair. Some tractors had the rear ends supported by blocks. Others were completely in half, while an engine was being installed. It was organized chaos, but all part of the business plan.

I got to know a lot of different people who worked as hired hands on the farm or mechanics in the shop. As the machinery business grew, the farming operation became less important. The garage was outgrown and the new shop was built. The business was firmly established. New and used farm machinery now filled lots on both sides of Race Street.

Carl was always on the go. While he was on buying expeditions, Margaret kept things going around the house. What a team they were then, just like today. Their family was growing, so I had some playmates. Every day I went to the farm or shop, looking for something to do. My mother used to get really upset when I would come home smelling like the silo or manure. Greasy pants from the shop weren't too good either, but what an interesting and active life I experienced around the Wengers!

Because there was so much machinery around, I thought all farms had a tractor hooked up to the feed wagon, another tractor for hay baling, another tractor hooked up to the harvester, and a different tractor to pull the wagons from the field to the farm. Of course, later in life I found that was not the case.

Although the work was long and hard, Carl saved his Saturday night for Hershey Bears hockey games. He and Margaret were big fans as season ticket holders. Occasionally, they would invite me along to the games. How exciting! Their oldest son, Lloyd, and I would travel around the Hershey Arena, checking things out. What great fun!

My family did not have a telephone in the early 1950s. My oldest brother (Carl's classmate) was in the Navy at the time. When he would travel home on leave, he would call the Wengers and they would relay my brother's schedule to our family. Great neighbors!

When I returned home from the Navy in 1973, jobs were scarce. Also, I was decompressing from Navy life and did not really pursue a 40 hour/week job. I went to see Carl and asked if he might have something for me to do. Of course he did. For a few months I did odd jobs around the shop and farm. Such is his understanding and caring attitude toward people.

In July 2008, I accidentally fell off my house roof. One of the first get well cards I received was from Carl and Margaret. They are still my neighbors.

Along with Carl's love of business was his love of his family, friends, and community. He provides opportunities for his children to pursue hobbies. Because there was always a lot of wheeled machinery around, it is not surprising that one of his children got into racing. Davey, their fifth child, benefitted from Carl's enthusiasm as a race fan. Carl provided shop space for the team and good cars for the track.

Most importantly, though, the racing was a good learning experience about dealing with the ups and downs of life. Win one night (GREAT!), crash the next (not so great). They had great teamwork among a group of hard-working young men. Carl appreciated and supported their enthusiasm.

Carl is a wonderful man. Loving, generous, caring, benevolent, friendly, demanding, insightful, and helpful. Best wishes always, Carl.

Jon P. Swanger, Former Neighbor, Friend, Bethel, Pa.

My memories of Carl and his family go back to when I was 10-15 years old. Helping on their dairy farm was a highlight of my life. I remember milking cows, carrying milk buckets to the milk house, putting hay and straw down the hay hole for the cattle. Scraping manure out of barn gutters also was an experience! I just liked to help Carl and Margaret.

I remember when Carl acquired his black 88 Oldsmobile Fastback auto. What a beauty that car was! I'm sure it helped him snatch up Margaret. She was always so pleasant and very nice to talk to, very good looking also. The children all turned out to be very congenial and great additions to the family. These memories and lots of others come to my mind often during my stay on this earth. I learned a lot from Carl and Margaret during my formative years.

Ken Wagner, Myerstown COB member, Owner of C.J. Wagner, Inc., Myerstown, Pa.

I have known Carl for many years to be a caring, generous, and honest individual. He has served his community in many ways.

All of Carl's properties are regularly maintained and litter free. One day, Carl was driving down King Street and noticed litter at the edge of one of his fields. He stopped his car and picked up the litter. In doing so, he accidentally stepped into a hole, injuring his leg. Carl had to spend that night in the hospital recovering from his mishap. He even involved the public by placing signs "Nice People Don't Litter," and we believe that has made a difference in our community.

After two tractor trailers rolled over on a dangerous curve south of Myerstown on Route 501, Carl pressured the state to install "dangerous curve arrow" signs to help prevent further injuries and accidents. Signs were installed in short order, and it proved successful.

One evening, Carl and some friends attended a car racing event in Reading area, where he lost his wallet. The next day, he received a phone call from a woman, whose son had found the wallet, and she told him where to pick it up. Upon receiving the wallet, Carl saw that the personal items and cash were still in place, so he gave all the cash that was in it to the boy to reward him for his honesty.

Whenever a fire occured in Eastern Lebanon County area, the following morning Carl would send employees and equipment to help clean up at no cost to the victims. In November 1983, several days before Thanksgiving, we returned home to my father's house, where we were living at the time, to find it burning. The next morning, Carl called me to offer a house owned by his one son for us to live in and a large garage for storage until our house was finished being built. We lived there several months. Carl has been very generous to us, as well as the Myerstown Fire Company and other community organizations.

Bernard W. Webber, Myerstown Lions Club Member, Lebanon, Pa.

Carl owns some land and a large cabin a few miles north of Bethel along Route 501. Each year in the fall, the Lions Club would have a "Steak Night" at Carl's cabin. Most times at least 20 Lions and their wives attended. It was very kind of Carl and Margaret to provide such a nice place for this event. They probably had a lot of work to prepare before and clean up afterwards. This was one of the most enjoyable events of the Lions Club for at least 15 years.

Grady W. Weeks, Friend, Business Associate, Ocala, Fla.

Carl has always stood out as a very organized businessman when he has attended our auctions at Weeks Auction Company. He always carried a three-inch-thick stack of cards in his shirt pocket, containing all types of information concerning tractors and equipment. He always knew the value of equipment because he not only carried the cards, he studied them.

Carl always wears a large cowboy hat and an equally large smile on his face. We have met all of his children and most all of his family because he is so proud of his family (and has every right to be because they are just as loving and respectful and business-minded as he is). There have been some tragedies in his life, but instead of turning sour he has turned them into charitable organizations to help others. My thoughts of Carl Wenger are good thoughts all the way around. His friendship is a real treasure.

C. Walter Whitmoyer, Jr., Friend, Myerstown, Pa.

I did not know Carl very well in high school because he was four years my senior. However, after I returned to Lebanon County following graduation from law school, I did get to know him well as an attorney and as a co-investor in a real estate investment corporation.

Carl is a visionary, an excellent salesman, and someone who knew how to build a business. I enjoyed our legal adventures together; there was never a dull moment, and we had some fun along the way.

Carl can be very persevering and works toward his goals even though achieving those goals may take time and be difficult. I believe the transition of his business interests to his family is a testament to his perseverance and his skill in achieving complex goals.

I have always found him thoughtful, conscientious, and someone who worried about doing the right thing. Among those "right things" was his interest in philanthropic activities. The Wenger Foundation is the culmination and final expression of his interest in making the community where he lives a better place. Indeed, the world is better because of John and Bertha having Carl as their only child.

Ken and Janet Winebark Family, Friends, Lindale, Texas

For the Winebark family, our relationship with the Wengers was a family affair, whether it was playing football with the grandsons; showing cattle with son, Glenn; or enjoying the love, fellowship, and friendship of Carl and Margaret. When I came to Lebanon County as the new County Extension Agent in the mid-1980s the Wenger name preceded the faces, as Wenger was synonymous with agriculture. We soon came to understand

why, as we quickly saw their support through not only production agriculture suppliers of equipment to local farmers, but
their giving heart through Farm-City events and 4-H and FFA
activities. I personally will never forget the times when at the
end of a 4-H/FFA livestock sale, Carl would announce that he
wanted to see all those youth whose animals didn't sell as well
do better. So he would raise the price on all those at the bottom
end and pick up the tab.

Carl and Margaret's giving didn't stop with agriculture though.
As time progressed and the Lord took me (us) from being the
County Agent into leading the On-Fire Youth Ministry, Carl and
Margaret's support continued. The Wenger Foundation became a
rock solid supporter of ours in sharing Jesus with the unchurched
kids in the Lebanon Valley. This relationship continues and has
even built in strength over these past nearly 20 years.

Once again as the Lord transitioned us to serving him in agriculture missions with Mercy Ships around the world, we still enjoy
the financial support and love of the Wengers, as they have continued these past eight years as part of our support base. In addition
to that, they provide the use of their beautiful mountain cabin as
our home away from home when we come back from Texas to
Eastern Pennsylvania to raise support and visit friends.

Some of our greatest memories are surely from the Brethren
Disaster Relief Sales. There the Wengers could always be counted on. I will never forget the last auction we attended before
moving to Texas. Our daughter Janine wanted to buy the quilt
that was made by the ladies of our home church—Richland
Church of the Brethren—as a keepsake. The quilt, however,
didn't make it to auction before we had to leave, so we left her
bid with Carl and Margaret. Well, we found out at church the
next day that the Richland ladies' quilt was quite popular and
brought much more than the bid my daughter could afford. So
she was sad she didn't get it, but happy that it made good money
for the relief auction.

That afternoon, we received a phone call from Carl and Margaret. They wanted to talk with us. So we all went down for a visit. While there, they shared that the quilt Janine wanted brought more than her bid. We talked on about our leaving the area to serve with Mercy Ships and how hard it was going to be to leave all of our friends there. But we felt God's calling on our lives to share agriculture around the world. Before we left, Carl handed us a check to help with our missions support. Then he asked Margaret to get the other package. She returned with a box and handed it to Janine, our daughter. She opened it and found the quilt she had wanted to buy. Of course, a flood of emotions hit, which were promptly washed away by tears. Now that quilt was doubly special, because it was made by the lovely ladies of our church and it was given by friends. We truly know that friends are friends forever if the Lord's the Lord of them.

M. Grace Wolgemuth, Friend Since Childhood, Manheim, Pa.

Carl was always committed to his goals and values.

When we visited Carl and Margaret in Florida, Carl would call my husband, Clyde, and say, "Let's rutsch today," meaning go to an auction or just run around together. Carl always made it a point to treat the auction clerks with snacks (usually a trail mix and drinks), a practice that his son Dave still carries on today. Since my family (husband, Clyde, and sons, Bob and Dennis) began Wolgemuth Auction Service in 1955, Wengers of Myerstown has been a great supporter of our farm equipment sales.

Knowing Carl and Margie since Sunday school at Midway Church of the Brethren, "Our lives are richer in all the ways that matter."

John W. Zechman, President, Penn View Bible Institute, Friend, Beavertown, Pa.

It is my privilege to have become acquainted with Carl Wenger. Our first meeting was at a benefit banquet—the type of event that Carl has become known as an expert in organizing—but in this case he was attending a banquet organized by another. I was seated next to him at the table, and it wasn't long until we found some common interest about which to converse. I was raised on a farm and around machinery. He had established a business, buying and selling equipment, so our time together was very enjoyable.

My wife and I have had the privilege of visiting in Carl and Margaret's home while traveling in Florida. One time I had intended to take them out for a meal, but instead of me paying the bill it was Carl who insisted that he would cover the expenses.

Since our first meeting, Carl has become a donor to our ministry at Penn View Bible Institute, in Penns Creek, Pennsylvania. He has taken an interest in our students and staff. Again, this is the norm for Carl. He has a big heart and passion for the work of the Lord to go forward. I count him as a real friend. He is always congenial, approachable, and friendly. The size of his heart coincides with the size of his hat—BIG!

Joel H. Zinn, Friend, Business Associate, Fellow Rotarian, Myerstown, Pa.

My friendship with Carl began over 40 years ago. We got involved in various projects as Myerstown Lions Club members in the '60s. About the same time his firm became a valued insurance customer of our insurance agency. I formed a closed real estate corporation shortly thereafter, and Carl became one of our three stockholders. I am Lutheran, Carl is Brethren, but we both acknowledge the same Lord and Savior. I include this background as a basis for my observations of Carl's life and philosophy.

We all acknowledge that circumstances make up and change our life philosophies. None of us is the same person we were 60 years ago. Life changes how we respond to circumstance, how we perceive who we are and respond to things about us. But within us remain some very instinctive traits that don't change, but are applied in different directions. Saying that, I see Carl as a different person today than when I first knew him—not better or worse, but different in the wisdom life has brought to him.

Early on in our relationship Carl told me, "I work hard and I play hard." Boy, was he right in that. I did the same thing, but not as hard. What made us do that? Both of us know we have Type A personalities. Characteristically, that means we are ambitious, driven—sometimes to excess and sometimes at a cost. While that can be an inbred characteristic, it also can be motivated by some past experience. In Carl's case, I believe his high school experiences had something to do with it. He wasn't an athlete and didn't think of himself as college material. His parents' farm was important to him, and he worked hard at that. But I believe he might have had a lower sense of worth as he compared himself to some of his classmates. As a result, upon graduation, the fire in his soul began to burn and he was on his way to succeed in whatever he set out to do.

Many people view Carl as a successful business and family person, and rightly so. But his life hasn't been without adversity. As his business world grew, he was challenged financially at times. Growing pains are just that. And he anguished one time when the solvency of his business was challenged. But like a Phoenix rising from the ashes, Carl was not about to acknowledge defeat. With the strong will and determination in his soul, he persevered and brought back stability to his company and formed the basis for the future of a successful family business.

The death of his granddaughter was a tragedy that was hard to bear for the entire family. I am sure that the spiritual faith and perseverance that comes through adversity showed our community that the Wenger family is a success in many ways.

Carl and I share a common tie in that we were both principals of a family business. We had a number of conversations about perpetuation and what we thought was best for our children. Successfully perpetuating a family business is not an easy matter. It comes with many complex issues, many of which are not financial. Carl would probably agree that it brought more challenges to him than any other business decision he had to make. We all want the best for our children. It's not just the planning for your children's future, but the planning of yours as well. We talked about what it meant for us to let go and how we had to let our children make their own decisions without our interference.

It was at this point in Carl's life that he thought of retirement. But here was man who had no hobbies to speak of, didn't play golf or tennis, was used to dealing with the public every day and no longer was the "head man." He started to pack his lunch and his tools and walk out in the very back field of the business to take old tractors apart. When Carl told me he was doing this, I thought to myself, "Not for long." The next time I saw Carl he wasn't taking old tractors apart anymore; he was headed south to auctions, making more deals. Now the motivation wasn't just profit, but just the satisfaction of being the person he was meant to be. I don't believe Carl met God anew in a burning bush in that field, but I do believe that he was given direction for some other ventures in his life. He had a new perception of some values of life.

I don't know that I could have chosen a better business partner in our real estate corporation. In the 40-some years as a partner, he has never questioned my leadership; rather, he was always an encourager. He gave good advice when it was required and brought to the company his wisdom in working with people. Indeed, I was led to the right person when we formed the company.

Spiritually, Carl and I are on the same page. We've talked about what our church families have meant to us and how God has blessed us. We came to the realization that what we were given was only on loan and in our trust. It is from this discovery that Carl's generosity evolved. There are many church-affiliated and charitable events that Carl supports, but I also know that his kindness goes beyond the acknowledged events to those unspoken needs of others. The Wenger Foundation also is a testimony to his beliefs. It was important to Carl that the concept of giving was implanted in the hearts of his children. Indeed, it has been, and for him that is a part of his success. His present philosophy of giving sets an example for all to follow.

Finally, I would be remiss if I didn't recognize his wife, Margaret. Carl and I grew up in a generation where Mom stayed at home, raised the kids, supported Dad in his business and social schedule, and had little chance to have their own self-worth encouraged. With seven children to raise and having to support Carl's schedule, only the best of women could have endured. Margaret made many sacrifices, I am sure. As Type A's, we only realize that after the fact. This is not to imply that Carl hasn't loved Margaret, but he will acknowledge that she has as much to do with the success of the Wengers as he did.

William Allen Zulker, D. Min., Friend, Richland, Pa.

I first heard of Wengers of Myerstown when I moved to Lebanon County in 2005 and soon discovered what an important establishment it was. As I drove down Route 501 I saw all the machines on both sides of the road and wondered about the nature of the business. Then one day I met Mr. Wenger, who graciously received me in his office. Though we had just met, before long he was talking to me as though we had known each other all of our lives. He then took me on a personalized tour of the business facilities, giving me—a retired 82-year-old preacher—the attention one would give a prospective customer. When the tour was over, he insisted that we go to lunch together at a nearby restaurant, where his wife joined us. What an interesting conversation we had.

We have met on several occasions since then, and I have heard about the wonderful church and community services that Mr. and Mrs. Wenger—along with their business—have rendered through the years. It has become obvious to me, as to many others, that here are two wonderful people who have put their Christian faith into practice. Furthermore, their faith in Christ is demonstrated without apology at home, in their business, and in their church. What a wonderful example and challenge to us all.